WALK
WHAI

Paul Hannon

HILLSIDE

HILLSIDE GUIDES - ACROSS THE NORTH & BEYOND

The Uplands of Britain
- **THE HIGH PEAKS OF ENGLAND & WALES**
- **YORKSHIRE DALES, MOORS & FELLS**

Long Distance Walks
- **COAST TO COAST WALK** • **DALES WAY** • **CLEVELAND WAY**
- **WESTMORLAND WAY** • **FURNESS WAY**
- **BRONTE WAY** • **PENDLE WAY** • **NIDDERDALE WAY**
- **LADY ANNE'S WAY** • **TRANS-PENNINE WAY** • **CALDERDALE WAY**

Hillwalking - Lake District
- **LAKELAND FELLS - SOUTH** • **LAKELAND FELLS - EAST**
- **LAKELAND FELLS - NORTH** • **LAKELAND FELLS - WEST**

Circular Walks - Peak District
- **NORTHERN PEAK** • **EASTERN PEAK** • **CENTRAL PEAK**
- **SOUTHERN PEAK** • **WESTERN PEAK**

Circular Walks - Yorkshire Dales
- **HOWGILL FELLS** • **THREE PEAKS** • **MALHAMDALE**
- **WHARFEDALE** • **NIDDERDALE** • **WENSLEYDALE** • **SWALEDALE**

Circular Walks - North York Moors
- **WESTERN MOORS** • **SOUTHERN MOORS** • **NORTHERN MOORS**

Circular Walks - South Pennines
- **BRONTE COUNTRY** • **ILKLEY MOOR**
- **CALDERDALE** • **SOUTHERN PENNINES**

Circular Walks - Lancashire
- **BOWLAND** • **PENDLE & THE RIBBLE** • **WEST PENNINE MOORS**

Circular Walks - North Pennines
- **TEESDALE** • **EDEN VALLEY**

Yorkshire Pub Walks • **HARROGATE/WHARFE VALLEY**

City Theme Walks • **YORK WALKS**

- **YORKSHIRE DALES CYCLE WAY** • **WEST YORKSHIRE CYCLE WAY**
- **AIRE VALLEY BIKING GUIDE** • **CALDERDALE BIKING GUIDE**
- **WHARFEDALE BIKING GUIDE**

WayMaster Visitor Guides • **YORKSHIRE DALES**

Send for a detailed current catalogue and pricelist,
and also visit *www.hillsidepublications.co.uk*

WALKING COUNTRY

WHARFEDALE

Paul Hannon

HILLSIDE

HILLSIDE
PUBLICATIONS
12 Broadlands
Keighley
West Yorkshire
BD20 6HX

First published as two different books
Walks in Wharfedale (1985) and
Rambles in Wharfedale (1991)
Updated and extended 1996
9th impression 2003

© Paul Hannon 1996, 2003

ISBN 1 870141 41 5

Cover illustration:
Springtime above Kettlewell
Back cover: Linton; Kilnsey Crag; Bolton Abbey
(Paul Hannon/Hillslides Picture Library)

Page 1: The Wharfe at New House, Deepdale
Page 3: Great Whernside summit

Printed in Great Britain by
Carnmor Print
95-97 London Road
Preston
Lancashire
PR1 4BA

CONTENTS

INTRODUCTION..6

THE WALKS *(mileage in brackets)*

1	Simon's Seat *from Bolton Abbey* (8½).............	12
2	Threshfield & Linton (3½).................................	15
3	Hubberholme & Cray (5)................................	18
4	Grass Wood (5½)......................................	21
5	Old Cote Moor (6½)...................................	24
6	Capplestone Gate (7½)...............................	28
7	Langerton Hill (6)......................................	32
8	Trollers Gill (7½).......................................	36
9	Penyghent Gill (8).....................................	40
10	Moor End (5)...	43
11	Bolton Abbey (4½).....................................	46
12	Upper Littondale (5½)................................	49
13	Hebden Gill (3½).......................................	52
14	Strid Wood (5)..	55
15	Thorpe Fell Top (9)....................................	58
16	Great Whernside (6)...................................	63
17	Barden Moor (8)..	66
18	Cam Head (5¾)...	70
19	Lea Green (7)..	74
20	Hazlewood Moor (6)...................................	78
21	Burnsall (6¼)...	82
22	Skyreholme (7½).......................................	86
23	Langstrothdale (6).....................................	89
24	Langcliffe Edge (5¾)..................................	92
25	Buckden Pike (8½).....................................	96
26	Horse Head Pass (8)...................................	100
27	Mastiles Lane (7¾).....................................	104
28	Simon's Seat *from Appletreewick* (6½)...........	108
29	Grassington Moor (5¾)...............................	112
30	Grimwith Reservoir (4¼)..............................	115
31	Threshfield Moor (6)...................................	118
32	Birks Fell Ridge (11)...................................	121

WALK LOG...126

INDEX..128

INTRODUCTION

The subject of this book is the upper valley of the River Wharfe, from the boundary of the Yorkshire Dales National Park at Bolton Bridge to beyond Buckden: included is the quieter side valley of Littondale. Wharfedale is the most popular valley in the Dales, this being attributable not least of all to its accessibility. The West Yorkshire cities of Leeds and Bradford and their surrounding towns are but a modest distance away, and on summer weekends the banks of the river see as many sun-worshippers as ramblers.

The Wharfe's name originates from the Celtic meaning 'swift water', and this lovely river races for almost 30 miles from Beckermonds to Bolton Bridge before a rather more sedate run to join the Ouse near Selby. At Beckermonds the Wharfe is formed by the confluence of Oughtershaw and Greenfield Becks, which have themselves already covered some distance from the lonely heights of Cam Fell.

The Wharfe's major tributary is the Skirfare, which flows through - and sometimes beneath - its own dale, Littondale, to lose its identity near the famous landmark of Kilnsey Crag. Though Littondale has many characteristics of its big brother, it is separated by steep sided fells and its seclusion gives it an intimate, possibly even greater charm.

North of Kilnsey the valley floors are dead flat and never more than half a mile wide, and at a very clearly defined boundary the fells begin their majestic rise to numerous 2000-foot summits. At regular intervals their slopes are scored by crystal clear mountain becks which have a short lived but very joyful journey. While the higher tops display the gritstone features of peat groughs and ever moist terrain, the lower slopes show off the ever fascinating scars of gleaming limestone.

*The summit,
Simon's Seat*

6

The entrance to the dale is guarded by the huge gritstone portals of Barden Moor and Barden Fell. These extensive areas of rolling heather moorland face each other across the Wharfe, overlooking the finest wooded riverside paths between Bolton Abbey and Grassington. They are valued grouse shooting country, but are happily the subject of negotiated access agreements - see next page.

While the industry of the dale has always featured farming, the 19th century was the heyday of lead mining, which gave employment to many from within and outwith the dale. Small operations existed all over the place, though the greatest concentration was on Grassington Moor. Their remains are evident today in spoil heaps, ruined smelt mills and kilns, shafts and levels. While these small scale workings have in most cases blended back into their natural surroundings, the dale is blighted by the alarming scale of three limestone quarries: two of these are at least largely hidden from most passers-by.

Barden Moor and Barden Fell incorporate vast access areas negoti-ated with the Duke of Devonshire's estate. Walkers are free to roam over the upland areas subject to certain restrictions, and Walks 1, 15, 17, 20 and 28 take advantage of this facility. The main point is that the moors can be 'closed' on certain days when shooting takes place (though not Sundays) and also at times of high fire risk. Notices are posted at all access points, though disappointment can be avoided by ringing the estate office or a National Park Centre beforehand. Also worth knowing in advance is the fact that dogs are not allowed.

Barden Bridge

St. Michael's,
Hubberholme

Getting around

The area is normally approached from Skipton, which has good links by bus and train with points further afield. The nearest town down-valley, however, is Ilkey, which is also well served by bus and rail. It is from Skipton, however, that the main bus service up the dale is based, running to Grassington. Beyond here is only an infrequent service, supplemented in season by various weekend, bank holiday and occasional services. There is no main road up the dale, but 'B' roads come in from Skipton and Bolton Bridge. Above Grassington one single 'B' road runs up the dale and out from Buckden over towards Aysgarth in Wensleydale. With a little planning, a number of permutations can be created by linking different sections of the walks, either to create longer routes or to take advantage of public transport.

Using the guide

Each walk is self-contained, with essential information being followed by a simple map and concise description of the route. Dovetailed between this are useful notes of features along the way, and inter-spersed are illustrations which both capture the flavour of the walks and record the many items of interest. In order to make the instructions easier to follow, essential route description has been highlighted in bold type, while items in lighter type refer to historical asides and things to look out for: in this format you can

Boundary stone on Thorpe Fell,
looking to the obelisk
on Cracoe Fell

find your way more easily while still locating features of interest at the relevant point in the text. Please remember to obey legitimate signs encountered on your walks: rights of way can be opened, closed or diverted. On these occasions, official notices should take precedence over the guidebook.

The simple sketch maps identify the location of the routes rather than the fine detail, and whilst the route description should be sufficient to guide you around, an Ordnance Survey map is recommended. The route as depicted can easily be plotted on the relevant OS map. To gain the most from a walk, the remarkable detail of the 1:25,000 scale maps cannot be matched: they also serve to vary walks as desired, giving an improved picture of one's surroundings and the availability of linking paths. This area is fortunate in that just two Outdoor Leisure sheets give comprehensive coverage of the walks:

Sheet 2 - Yorkshire Dales South/West
(this was Sheet 10 - Yorkshire Dales South, prior to 1997 edition)
& Sheet 30 - Yorkshire Dales North/Central

Also extremely useful for general planning purposes are the Landranger sheets, at 1:50,000. The following cover the area:
98 - Wensleydale & Upper Wharfedale;
99 - Northallerton & Ripon; 103 - Blackburn & Burnley;
104 - Leeds, Bradford & Harrogate
(sheet 98 is the main one, covering over two-thirds of the walks)
In addition, Yorkshire Dales 1-inch Tourist Map covers the whole area.

Bolton Priory

SOME USEFUL ADDRESSES

Ramblers' Association
2nd Floor, Camelford House, 87-89 Albert Embankment, London SE1 7BR
Tel. 020-7339 8500

Yorkshire Dales National Park
Colvend, Hebden Road, Grassington, Skipton BD23 5LB
Tel. 01756-752748

Grassington National Park Centre
Hebden Road, Grassington BD23 5LB
Tel. 01756-752774

Tourist Information
35 Coach Street, **Skipton** Tel. 01756-792809
Station Road, **Ilkley**   Tel. 01943-602319

Bolton Abbey Estate office   Tel. 01756-710227

Yorkshire Dales Society
Civic Centre, Cross Green, Otley LS21 1HD
Tel. 01943-461938

Upper Wharfedale Folk Museum
6 The Square, Grassington
Tel. 01756-752800

The National Trust Regional Office
Goddards, 27 Tadcaster Road, York YO2 2QG
Tel. 01904-702021

Traveline - public transport information
Tel. 0870 608 2608

Rail services - National Enquiry Line
Tel. 0345-484950

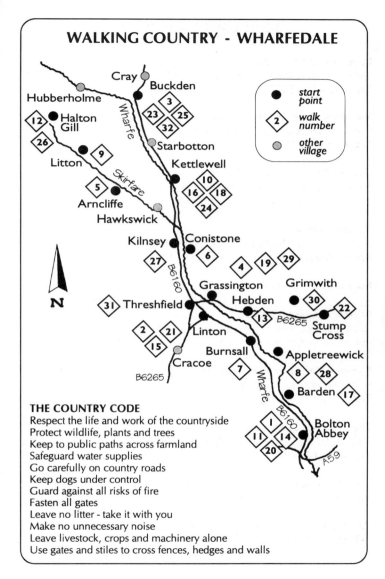

WALKING COUNTRY - WHARFEDALE

Cray
Buckden
Hubberholme
3
23 25
12 Halton
Gill   32
26   Starbotton
Litton   9   Kettlewell
5   10
Arncliffe   16 18
Hawkswick   24

Kilnsey Conistone
27   6
4 19 29
Grassington   Grimwith
31 Threshfield Hebden 30
13 B6265   22
2   21   Linton   Stump
15   Burnsall   Cross
Cracoe   7   Appletreewick
B6265   8 28
Barden 17

N

Wharfe
Skirfare
B6160
Wharfe
B6160
A59
Bolton
Abbey

start point
2 walk number
other village

THE COUNTRY CODE

Respect the life and work of the countryside
Protect wildlife, plants and trees
Keep to public paths across farmland
Safeguard water supplies
Go carefully on country roads
Keep dogs under control
Guard against all risks of fire
Fasten all gates
Leave no litter - take it with you
Make no unnecessary noise
Leave livestock, crops and machinery alone
Use gates and stiles to cross fences, hedges and walls

1

SIMON'S SEAT
from Bolton Abbey

START *Bolton Abbey*   *Grid ref. SE 077552*

DISTANCE *8½ miles*

ORDNANCE SURVEY MAPS
1:50,000
Landranger 104 - Leeds, Bradford & Harrogate
1:25,000
Outdoor Leisure 2 - Yorkshire Dales South/West

ACCESS *Start from the Cavendish Pavilion, signposted off the B6160 just north of Bolton Abbey, turning off by the large memorial fountain. There is a large car park. The B6160 is served by Skipton-Bolton Abbey-Grassington buses and by seasonal services including Dalesbus.*

A superb expedition through colourful country to a grand airy top. Excellent paths throughout. This is the only walk in the book to return by what is largely the same route, but it is grand!

• *IMPORTANT* The whole of this moorland is collectively known as Barden Fell, part of the Duke of Devonshire's estate. From shortly after leaving the road above Posforth Bridge we are on access land which may be closed on certain days during the grouse shooting season (not Sundays) and at times of high fire risk. Notices are posted at the access point, but for advance information, contact Grassington National Park Centre or the estate office. Dogs are not allowed on the access area.

❺ Leave the Pavilion by crossing the wooden bridge over the Wharfe and immediately taking a path upstream. Entering trees it soon emerges onto a narrow road at Posforth Bridge. Double back

12

up the hill to a clearing at the top, and forsake the road for a gate on the left by an access notice. **Head half-left across the pasture past some hoary oaks to a gate, from where a good track crosses to reach Posforth Gill in the Valley of Desolation.** Its title could not be less appropriate to the colourful terrain here, but it refers to the aftermath of a great storm in 1826. **While the main path turns right to run along the rim of the drop to the beck, a detour down to it repays with a close-up view of the waterfall.**

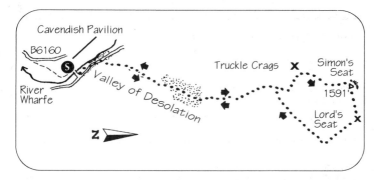

Having witnessed this spectacle the beck might be forded and the north bank followed upstream, though the regularly used path remains on the same side to cross by a tiny footbridge a little further up. Soon a fork is reached and our way rises to the left. However, by simply continuing upstream a short way an equally lovely waterfall can be enjoyed. **The main path, meanwhile, rises to a stile to enter Laund Pasture Plantation. A wide track leads rapidly to the far end of the trees, where a gate admits onto the open moor, a stirring moment.**

A good, clear track heads directly away, and leads unerringly to the summit of Simon's Seat. On the way there it fords Great Agill Beck prior to a short, steep section. At a stone table Truckle Crags and more distantly Simon's Seat come into view. **Beyond the table a shooters' track branches off to the right: this is where we rejoin the outward route on returning from the top. Our ascending path crosses the headwaters of the beck before swinging right to pass Truckle Crags, and the large grouping of rocks atop Simon's Seat is only a couple of minutes away.**

13

The environs of the summit are a source of potential confusion in bad visibility, but the presence of a footpath sign at the nearby path junction helps avoid this possibility. The unmistakable form of an Ordnance Survey column (S5294) adorns the highest rocks, and to add interest to the final few feet, hands must be used to attain it. The giant boulders of Simon's Seat and Lord's Seat make an ideal playground for scramblers, though the great walls of rock falling to the north from the summit are strictly the preserve of rock climbers.

The view from Simon's Seat is made unforgettable by virtue of our sheltered line of approach, keeping all to the north hidden until the very last moment. Along with the anticipated distant panorama is a dramatic bird's-eye view of the valley below, a result of the unbroken plunge of the northern slope of the fell. The environs of Skyreholme and Appletreewick form a splendid picture, with Trollers Gill, Parceval Hall and Grimwith Reservoir easily located. A nice section of the Wharfe itself can also be seen. See also the diagram on page 111.

To vary the return take the sketchy path heading east to the prominent outcrops of Lord's Seat, then turn right alongside the wall immediately behind. After a short half-mile of gradual descent turn sharp right onto a broad shooter's track. This now undulates across the moor and leads the way unfailingly back to the outward route near the stone table. Steps can now be happily retraced all the way back to the Pavilion.

The waterfall,
Posforth Gill

14

2

THRESHFIELD & LINTON

START Linton Falls   Grid ref. SE 001631

DISTANCE 3 miles

ORDNANCE SURVEY MAPS
1:50,000
Landranger 98 - Wensleydale & Upper Wharfedale
1:25,000
Outdoor Leisure 2 - Yorkshire Dales South/West

ACCESS Start from the National Park car park on the cul-de-sac road to Linton church. The walk can also be easily started from Grassington or Linton, both served by bus from Skipton.

A simple amble through the fields between mid-Wharfedale villages.

S **From the car park go back along the road for a short distance, and after the last house turn down to the right in a ginnel leading to a footbridge across the Wharfe.** This makes a fine vantage point as the river crashes loudly over a tangle of rock ledges and boulders. Still known by many as the 'Tin Bridge', the old iron structure (itself not the original metal bridge) was replaced by a modern wooden edifice in 1989.

After surveying the scene turn back a few yards to cross the little pack-bridge over a similarly tiny stream. Now pass to the right of the cottage to accompany the Wharfe upsteam. Here is a dramatic contrast as the river flows wide and calm between two weirs. Grassington Bridge is in view upstream. **Soon the path is channeled up to a stile onto a road. Now turn left the short distance to Threshfield school.** This fine old building dates from the 17th century, having originally been a grammar school.

Take a gate immediately after the schoolyard and head up the field on a track which swings right to a bridge across the former railway line. The railway was a branch line from Skipton to Grassington, and was in use from 1902 to 1969. It still comes within a couple of miles, but only to serve the quarry. **The track then continues away from it to run a little sketchily to a gate onto another road. Turn right then first left to enter the centre of old Threshfield.**

Threshfield is a disjointed village scattered in various directions around the junction of the Skipton-Grassington road with the main updale road. The 'new' part of the village - with its striking Catholic church of modern design - is along the road towards Grassington, but it is the more interesting old corner we visit. Solid stone cottages and farm buildings overlook a quaint, triangular green, enclosed by walls and shrouded in trees. Inside are some stocks and the flowers of spring. On turning alongside the green note the stone lintel of the old post office, dated 1651. Just across the main road is the popular *Old Hall* inn, whose title serves to indicate its original purpose. Passed earlier in the walk, of course, was the village school.

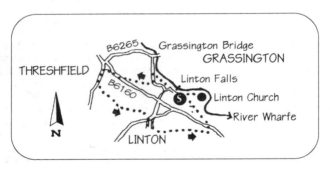

At the end of the road turn left to join the main road as it descends to Threshfield Bridge. Immediately after the buildings on the other side escape by a stile on the left to rise diagonally up the field to a gateway. Follow the wall away from it to pass through a tree-fringed wall, then continue straight across the next field to a footbridge back over the former railway line. Bear half-right down the field to a wall corner shrouded in trees, where a gate gives access to an enclosed track. Running parallel with Linton Beck to the left, it leads unfailingly to the road through Linton village.

Linton is one of northern England's most attractive villages. A rich assortment of limestone buildings stand in very laid-back fashion, none wishing to crowd the spacious green. Nearest is the white-washed little hostelry, whose name recalls a local benefactor. Richard Fountaine made his money in London, but in his will he remembered Linton by paying for the 'hospital' at the end of the green. This 18th century building remains in use as almshouses. Through the green runs Linton Beck, crossed in quick succession by a road bridge, a ford, a clapper bridge and most strikingly, a packhorse bridge.

Turn briefly right and then sharp left between the green and the *Fountaine Inn*. A choice of beck crossings conveys us to the opposite lane, which is followed to the right to its demise. Here turn left in front of a barn and along a short enclosed track. Soon it breaks free, and is rapidly vacated by means of a stile on the left. Stay with the left hand wall until it begins to drop away, then contour round to the right: down to the left now is a former residential school. On reaching a cross-wall, the first of four stiles on virtually the same contour is encountered. After the last of these, hidden in a corner, drop down to the left to a gate onto the Threshfield-Burnsall road again. The fields hereabouts - and across the river - sport the well defined strip lynchets, cultivation terraces of the Anglian farmers.

Turn right along the road a few yards to a gate opposite, then head diagonally across two narrow fields with gap-stiles. Continue the direction to near the top corner of a plantation, but remain above the steep drop towards Linton church and the river, instead going across to the far corner of the field. A stile will be found to the right of a barn: from it continue on through a meadow to its far corner, there joining a short, enclosed way emerging back onto the road. Before returning to the car park, turn right to visit the church of St. Michael and all Angels, so positioned as to be central to the several villages it was built to serve. Dating from Norman times, it retains much 15th century work and its lovely interior lives up to its idyllic setting.

St. Michael's, Linton

3

HUBBERHOLME & CRAY

START *Buckden*   *Grid ref. SD 942772*

DISTANCE *5 miles*

ORDNANCE SURVEY MAPS
1:50,000
Landranger 98 - Wensleydale & Upper Wharfedale
1:25,000
Outdoor Leisure 30 - Yorkshire Dales North/Central

ACCESS *Start from the village centre. There is a large National Park car park. Buckden is served by occasional bus from Skipton via Grassington, and by seasonal services such as Dalesbus.*

A classic promenade round the valley head, full of variety and interest.

S Buckden is the first sizeable settlement encountered by the Wharfe, and stands at the meeting place of two high roads from Wensleydale to the north. The good quality B6160 comes via Cray to take over as the valley road from the narrow, winding strip of tarmac that reaches nearly 2000 feet on its way over Fleet Moss from Hawes, before running through Langstrothdale to Buckden. In medieval times Buckden was the centre of a vast hunting forest, and its hostelry recalls its former importance in its name. The village stands high above the river on the slopes of Buckden Pike, and swift-flowing Buckden Beck carves a deep defile down from the summit.

Leave the car park not by its exit, instead use a gate at its northern end from where a stony track gently rises up Buckden Rake. To the left the upper dale leads to moorland heights, with the Birks Fell ridge behind. **At the end of the surround of trees it turns right through a gate to commence a pleasant, level section. On drawing level with**

the buildings of Cray down to the left, take a gate in the adjacent wall and drop down a steep field to another gate from where Cray Gill is forded to join the road right next to the inn.

Situated at over 1000 feet above sea level, the farming hamlet of Cray is the last outpost of Wharfedale on the high road over to Bishopdale and ultimately Wensleydale. This crossing of the fells is known as the Kidstones Pass, and is the easiest motorable escape out of the valley north of Grassington. Cray's one amenity is the *White Lion*, an uncomplicated and welcoming hostelry with a flagged floor.

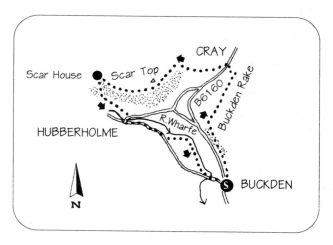

To leave Cray take the farm track immediately behind the hostelry and follow it up to the left, keeping to the right of the various farm buildings. Having passed through a gate above the last building the way remains level through several fields, becoming indistinct but aiming for a barn just ahead. Go to the left of it to then swing right to a tiny footbridge over Crook Gill. The walk from Crook Gill to Scar House is along the short-cropped turf of Scar Top, above a steep drop through ancient woodlands. The scarp is marked by limestone scars and sections of pavement. The slopes to the north rise more steadily to the height of 2109ft on the largely unfrequented Yockenthwaite Moor. From Cray to Scar House we are treated to superlative views down the length of the dale.

From the footbridge swing left to commence a long, easy mile above the well-defined escarpment cloaked in trees on the left: part-way along, the stately Wharfedale Cairn beckons just up to the right. Sentinel of the upper valley and highest point of the walk at 1180ft, this solidly built edifice is a notable landmark in many local views. **All too soon the path arrives just above isolated Scar House.** Restored last century, it was the scene of early Quaker gatherings. **Turn down between the buildings to accompany the stony access road down the hillside into Hubberholme, emerging alongside the church.**

Barely even a hamlet, Hubberholme boasts two famous buildings and a shapely bridge which connects them. The church of St. Michael is a gem, its tower showing Norman traces. Its best feature is a 500-year old oak rood loft, one of only two remaining in Yorkshire, while some pews bear the famous trademark of 'Mousy' Thompson. Carving therefore - both ancient and modern - dominates the interior of this highest church in the dale. Outside, meanwhile, the sparkling Wharfe runs almost past its very door. Across the river is the whitewashed and homely *George Inn* in an idyllic setting. Formerly housing the vicar, its flagged floors continue to be the scene of the New Year 'land-letting' when proceeds of a 'poor pasture' go to needy parishioners.

For the final leg of the walk cross the bridge over the Wharfe to the inn, and turn left along the road. After about half a mile take a gate on the left to rejoin the river, which is now accompanied down-dale to soon reach Buckden Bridge. Join the road to re-cross the river back into the village.

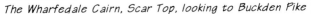

The Wharfedale Cairn, Scar Top, looking to Buckden Pike

4

GRASS WOOD

START *Grassington*   *Grid ref. SE 002639*

DISTANCE *5½ miles*

ORDNANCE SURVEY MAPS
1:50,000
Landranger 98 - Wensleydale & Upper Wharfedale
1:25,000
Outdoor Leisure 2 - Yorkshire Dales South/West

ACCESS *Start from the square in the village centre. There is a large National Park car park by the information centre on the Hebden road. Grassington is served by bus from Skipton.*

A walk of two distinct halves, on good paths through woodland and by riverbank.

S Grassington is the undisputed 'capital' of the upper Wharfedale area, a thriving community with a good range of facilities. The fine, cobbled square is the focal point but it is really only the shop window: hidden away is enough interest for a day's leisurely exploration. Historically, Grassington boasted an 18th century theatre and a lead mining industry of which its nearby moor still displays much evidence. The many buildings of character include the Old Hall and the former Town Hall-cum-institute. Here also is the Upper Wharfedale Folk Museum and the headquarters of the fell rescue organisation and the National Park.

From the cobbled square head up the main street past the *Devonshire Arms* as far as a crossroads next to the institute. Here turn left along Chapel Street. Part way along, turn up Bank Lane on the right: this quickly swings left to level out as a walled track. Open views look to Grass Wood and the limestone pasures ahead. **At a bend take a**

small gate on the left, and cross a field centre to a stile. Turn left down a brow to a stile on the right, with a rough track below (coming from Town Head). Here cross to a stile in the opposite wall in front, and bear right across the field to a stile onto an enclosed track (Cove Lane). Accompany it to its demise then take the right-hand of two facing gates to follow a wall in the same direction. At the field end cross to a ladder-stile which admits to Grass Wood. Although graced with much wooded beauty, Grass Wood is also of major importance in the botanical world, a bewildering variety of flowers being found here. It is run by the Yorkshire Wildlife Trust. Its counterpart Bastow Wood reaches greater altitudes to the right of our path. Just after entering the wood we pass the site of a settlement of Celtic origin.

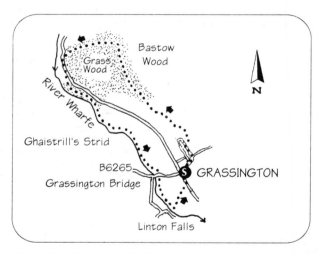

A good path heads up through the trees, rising steadily for about half a mile. After levelling out, two narrower paths branch right in quick succession, followed by a slight descent to a flat clearing where several tracks meet. Although this widest track we are currently on will drop down to meet the definitive path, our route proper involves retracing the few yards back to the second of those aforementioned narrower branches passed on the way to the clearing. It maintains a level course through the trees with a moss covered limestone pavement on the left, before dropping down towards the far end of the wood.

22

For a spell there are splendid views north to Kilnsey Crag, Buckden Pike and the river. **After a sharp left turn it descends more gently, merging into the wide track forsaken earlier before emerging at a stile onto Grass Wood Lane.** Here stood the gibbet that hanged Tom Lee, local blacksmith turned notorious murderer two centuries ago.

Head left along this quiet back road for a short distance and take a stile into the trees on the right. The main path sets a course for the Wharfe's bank, which is accompanied downstream firstly through trees and then green pastures. The large building high on the opposite bank is Netherside Hall, now a school. **A cluster of trees marks the position of Ghaistrill's Strid, like Linton Falls still to come, a rare moment of turbulence for the Wharfe. From here a string of stiles in quick succession precede more green pastures to arrive at Grassington Bridge.**

Cross the road here to pass below a row of houses before regaining the same bank of the river. Two weirs are passed before arriving at the less uniform delights of Linton Falls. Here the Wharfe crashes loudly over a tangle of rock ledges and boulders, and is viewed dramatically from the footbridge just above. Still known by many as the 'Tin Bridge', the old iron structure was replaced by a modern edifice in 1989. New houses have replaced the former mill on the opposite bank. **After surveying the scene conclude the walk by turning up the narrow snicket (the 'Snake Walk') on our bank, which with good views of Linton church returns us to the main car park.**

Grassington Bridge

5

OLD COTE MOOR

START Arncliffe   Grid ref. SD 931718

DISTANCE 6½ miles

ORDNANCE SURVEY MAPS
1:50,000
Landranger 98 - Wensleydale & Upper Wharfedale
1:25,000
Outdoor Leisure 2 - Yorkshire Dales South/West
                    30 - Yorkshire Dales North/Central

ACCESS Start from the village green, parking tidily alongside, or by the bridge by the church. Served by a schoolday bus only. A popular alternative is to start from Kettlewell, with a slightly better bus service from Skipton/Grassington.

An inter valley crossing on delightful paths. Excellent views. Less than two miles below Hawkswick the Skirfare merges with the Wharfe, and during this walk we are treated to unparalleled vistas of substantial lengths of these twin-like dales immediately above their confluence. In both cases flat valley floors give way to equally well-defined slopes.

⑤ Arncliffe is one of the most attractive yet least spoilt villages in the Dales, and is regarded as the 'capital' of Littondale. A variety of characterful greystone houses stand back in relaxed manner from a spacious green. The unpretentious inn, the *Falcon*, maintains this mood, and is the only hostelry in the area to serve its ale in that unrivalled fashion, directly from the barrel.

Out of sight of the green is the church of St.Oswald, which has found its own niche embowered in trees in a truly beautiful riverside setting. Though largely rebuilt last century, the solid tower dates back 500 years. Inside is a list of the Littondale men who marched off to fight at Flodden Field in 1513. Across the shapely bridge, the house at Bridge End played host to Charles Kingsley during his *Water Babies* period.

From the village green take the Litton (up-dale) road, past the church and across the bridge over the Skirfare. At once leave the road by the stile on the right to accompany the river downstream, but only a short distance to another stile onto a narrow road. From the stile opposite a good path rises diagonally through two fields to enter Byre Bank Wood. This is an ancient pocket of woodland happily left unfelled due to its steepness. As a result it supports some rarely seen plant life. **The path continues up through the trees to leave by negotiating the modest Pot Scar at the top.** Looking back, a major feature is the deep-cut Cowside Beck just behind Arncliffe.

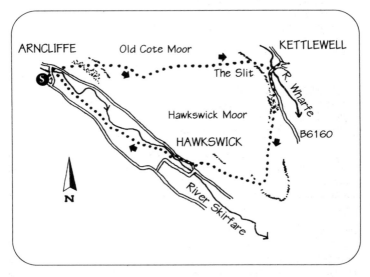

Maintaining the same course, the path resumes in easier vein: at a gateway in a collapsing wall a short level section precedes the final pull, and at the second of a pair of neighbouring stiles the ridge-wall on Old Cote Moor is gained. Buckden Pike dominates the scene ahead, with uniform looking villages at its foot. Great Whernside, as ever, rises protectively above Kettlewell.

Descent to Kettlewell commences immediately, the slightly less clear path inclining right to eventually locate a stile in a wall descending from the moor top. Continuing down at a similar angle a plateau briefly interrupts the drop before squeezing through the 'Slit', a well used way through a narrow band of limestone. The path then drops down to merge with another before reaching a gate onto the road at the entrance to Kettlewell. The route now lies along to the right, though weighing up the prospect of an immediate return climb against the pubs and cafes of Kettlewell, few will resist the opportunity to break journey here.

Kettlewell is the hub of the upper dale, a junction of roads and natural halting place. It stands on what was a major coaching route to Richmond, and the two inns at the entrance to the village would have serviced the weary travellers. The route in question is now a surfaced road, but still provides a tortuous way over into Coverdale. Shops, tearooms a third pub and plentiful accommodation - including a youth hostel - add more life to a village being steadily engulfed by holiday homes. Kettlewell straddles its own beck which largely drains the slopes of Great Whernside, very much Kettlewell's mountain. These slopes bear the scars of lead mining, the one-time industry now replaced by tourism as a partner to farming. Some delectable cottages and gardens line the beck as it races through the village.

On leaving the village return over the bridge and follow the road a short distance as far as a gate and footpath sign pointing up to the right. A good path heads away, bearing right at a fork and then rising

Looking down Wharfedale from Knipe Scar: Barden Moor beyond Kilnsey Crag

through trees to a level enclosure. **Bearing up to the right beneath a pinewood a stile will be found in the top corner of the field, with another one just above it. The path then rises through a low scar and continues climbing steadily to a cairn marking the highest point of this crossing.** This lower ridge crossing on Hawkswick Moor permits some intimate views down Wharfedale.

From the cairn the path undulates across to a stile in the ridge wall. Just beyond is another cairn from where the path turns sharply right to begin its descent into Littondale. A nice, easy drop down concludes by entering Hawkswick enclosed by walls. Hawkswick is the Skirfare's last village, and being the only one off the 'main' up-dale road it remains wonderfully undisturbed. **Turn right past the houses to arrive at a footbridge, and on crossing it take a stile on the right to accompany the Skirfare upstream.**

This level return to Arncliffe is fairly straightforward, with an assortment of stiles and gates to point the way. For the most part the river keeps its distance, but it returns for the last third of a mile to usher us back into the village, a gate by a barn preceding a short drive emerging by the church.

St. Oswald's,
Arncliffe

6

CAPPLESTONE GATE

START *Conistone*   *Grid ref. SD 980674*

DISTANCE *7½ miles*

ORDNANCE SURVEY MAPS
1:50,000
Landranger 98 - Wensleydale & Upper Wharfedale
1:25,000
Outdoor Leisure 2 - Yorkshire Dales South/West

ACCESS *Start from the village centre. Parking is fairly limited: there is more room on the wide section of road towards the bridge. An alternative start is the B6160 at Kilnsey. This is served by occasional Grassington-Buckden buses and seasonal Dalesbus.*

An intimate exploration of limestone country at its best - with a surprise at the top. The going is everywhere easy - not to be missed.

S Conistone is an attractive little village avoided by the main road which heads up-dale just half a mile distant, across the river at Kilnsey: even from this distance the famous crag loses none of its grandeur. Every piece of stone in Conistone's cottages matches the natural landscape of the village's hinterland. Though restored a century ago, the hidden church of St. Mary retains some Norman features.

From the main road junction set off along the Kettlewell road, and immediately turn right on a track across a wide 'green'. From the gate at the far end bear right between two old caravans, a clear path materialising and becoming stony underfoot as it heads up the dry valley of Conistone Dib. After being tightly confined by the imposing buttresses of Gurling Trough the path emerges into the open to pass through a long, green pasture. When the slopes close in again stay with the wall for a short, stony climb to the head of the valley.

Conistone Dib is a classic example of a dry limestone valley, narrowing to very distinctive rock-girt termini. **At the very top the wall is crossed by a stile as it abuts onto a cliff: just above take a stile on the right, and then turn left on a track to a gate which gives access to the wide track of the Bycliffe Road.** A superb limestone pavement sits just above: at its far side is an old limekiln. Up the slope meanwhile, the Ordnance column at the summit of the walk can already be discerned.

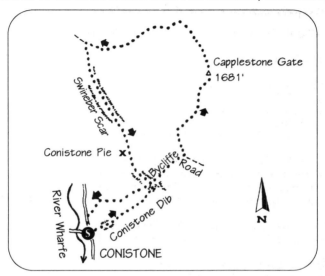

Turn right along the Bycliffe Road, and shortly after becoming enclosed leave by a gate on the left just as it bends sharp right. The Bycliffe Road, incidentally, is an old peat road which continues to lonely Mossdale. **A tractor track crosses the field towards a small plantation, passing to the right of it.** Our route here is the Conistone Turf Road, bound for the peaty ground above the limestone limit. **The track climbs to the far end of a prominent scar, and from a gateway rises more gently to approach the OS column at 1681ft on Capplestone Gate.**

After the wonders of dazzling limestone it comes as a surprise to meet the sombre gritstone of Capplestone Gate. If our goal had been a hundred feet lower we would not have left limestone, but this

29

dramatic transformation at the 1600ft contour gives us a stroll among boulders and old mine workings in complete contrast to the rest of the journey. Capplestone Gate is a highly extensive viewpoint, arguably the best all round vantage point for the varied Wharfedale scene. The fell country to the west includes, clockwise; Simon's Seat, Thorpe Fell Top, Cracoe Fell, Pendle Hill, Parson's Pulpit, Fountains Fell, Penyghent, Plover Hill, Birks Fell, Yockenthwaite Moor, Buckden Pike and Great Whernside, of which our viewpoint is a shoulder.

After a well earned rest resume by taking the stile by the gate and turning left along a sketchy path which remains close to the wall running along the bottom edge of the moor. An area rich in relics of the mining industry is encountered, followed by some modest gritstone outcrops. When the wall returns a solid cairn is passed, and a little further a stile in the wall is used to leave the moor. On surmounting it, the whole world seems to appear at one's feet.

St. Mary's, Conistone

After an initially steep descent the path drops leisurely through a collapsed wall and on through a long pasture. At a sketchy fork bear left, and remaining in the same pasture bear right near the bottom to leave by a gate near the corner. At this gate comes the first real valley view of the walk, with the environs of Kettlewell prominent. **A track then descends half-right towards a gate into a plantation.**

Do not enter the trees, but turn sharp left on a path which bears to the right of an increasing scar to commence a long, level section. A stile in a cross-wall is the first of five to be encountered. Here at

30

Looking back to Conistone Pie

this first stile the fortress-like Conistone Pie appears directly ahead. Across the valley is the often dark shadow of Kilnsey Crag, backing the secretive Amerdale Dub, confluence of Skirfare with Wharfe (Amerdale is the old name for Littondale).

Although the path is not always clear underfoot, the route is in no doubt. The final stile is adjacent to Conistone Pie. This minor upthrust of rock crowned by a cairn is a conspicuous Wharfedale landmark. It commands a superb view of the fork of the arrow-like valleys of the Wharfe and Skirfare. **Beyond here another scar materialises to usher us back to rejoin the Bycliffe Road above Conistone Dib.**

Now turn right along it - now as Scot Gate Lane - soon descending Wassa Bank past the T.V. mast which has been in sight at various stages of the walk. Becoming surfaced, the access road leads down to join the Conistone-Kettlewell road, with the village only minutes along to the left.

On Conistone Pie, looking to Old Cote Moor dividing Littondale and Upper Wharfedale

LANGERTON HILL

START *Burnsall*   *Grid ref. SE 032611*

DISTANCE *6 miles*

ORDNANCE SURVEY MAPS
1:50,000
Landranger 98 - Wensleydale & Upper Wharfedale
1:25,000
Outdoor Leisure 2 - Yorkshire Dales South/West

ACCESS *Start from the village centre. There is a sizeable car park at the entrance to the village, added to which a riverside meadow is often opened up to supplement it. Burnsall is served by Skipton-Bolton Abbey-Grassington buses and seasonal Dalesbus.*

A circuit of Barben Beck over gently rolling hills, with a fine stretch of the Wharfe to finish.

S Burnsall's setting is one of near perfection, with bridge, green, inn, maypole, church and cottages fusing into an unforgettable Wharfedale scene. Be sure to walk up the road from the *Red Lion* to St.Wilfred's church which dates largely from the 15th century and has an inscribed Norman font. Note also the functional lych-gate. Alongside is the village school, founded in 1602 by William Craven as one of the earliest grammar schools.

Leave Burnsall by crossing the bridge and using the steps on the left to descend to the river. After two stiles near the river climb directly up the very steep field to a stile onto the narrow Skuff Road. A splendid retrospective view is now earned of Burnsall backed by its fell. **From the stile opposite climb another field to a stile and on to another in the very corner ahead. Now rise diagonally across a large**

32

field to a stile onto another road. Turn up it only as far as a sharp bend, and leave by a stile directly ahead. After a continual rise up the sides of two fields, the brow of Langerton Hill is gained just below its highest point.

For its modest altitude of 912ft, Langerton Hill is an extensive viewpoint. At the top end of Wharfedale are the summits of Buckden Pike and Great Whernside, with Simon's Seat and Burnsall Fell dominating the immediate vicinity. To the west are the heights beyond Malham and those of Malham Moor. Note also the dam of Grimwith Reservoir.

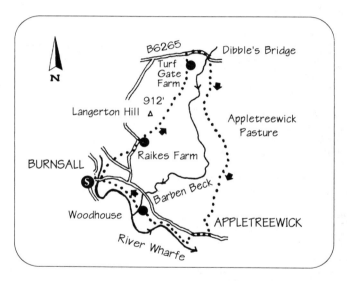

Our route, meanwhile, resumes its original direction from the last stile and continues to follow the right-hand wall away to a stile in it. Remain near the wall to descend a large field to a tiny stream at the far end. From the stile behind it rise half right to a stile near a barn, then accompany the right-hand wall up to another barn. From two neighbouring stiles continue with the wall now on the left to arrive at Turf Gate Farm. Head straight on past all the buildings to follow its access road out onto the Grassington-Pateley Bridge road. Turn right along the road to drop down to Dibble's Bridge.

33

This dangerous spot was the scene of a tragic coach crash in 1975. A mile north of Dibble's Bridge is Grimwith Reservoir (see WALK 30), which supplies Bradford. Between the reservoir and the bridge the watercourse is not Barben Beck, but the River Dibb. Covering only one mile under this guise, is it the shortest river in the country?

Immediately after crossing the bridge a stile gives access to a beckside area of limestone outcrops. Vacate it by a stile in the far top corner, and continue along to a gate directly ahead. Advance straight across to a stile ahead to enter the untamed expanse of Appletreewick Pasture sloping down to Barben Beck. A tiny beck across our path is followed by a long, level section on a reasonably clear route high above the beck.

When a wall appears in front the path fades, but simply deflect left of it to suddenly be confined by stone walls. Escape along a short, narrow passage on the left, and on emerging turn right with the wall to eventually join an enclosed track across our way. Cross straight over to enter another long, narrow pasture, and by the opposite corner a wide track has materialised. It now gets enclosed by walls to soon drop down onto the road at one end of Appletreewick village, rather conveniently adjacent to one of its two hostelries.

Appletreewick has several claims to fame, even though many visitors may best remember its delightful name. Here are three halls and two inns in amongst a wonderful assortment of cottages. All stand on or about the narrow road wandering through the village, from the three-storeyed High Hall at the top - note the tiny St. John's church nearby - to Low Hall with its gabled porch at the very bottom. Probably the oldest however is the curiously named Mock Beggar Hall, a fine little edifice that once went by the title of Monk's Hall.

The bridge, Burnsall

Of the two hostelries, the *Craven Arms* takes its name from the family of William Craven, a Dick Whittington character who found his fortune in London, becoming Lord Mayor in 1611. Not forgetting his beginnings he became a worthy local benefactor, having Burnsall's grammar school and a number of bridges in the district built. The *New Inn*, meanwhile, achieved national fame in the 1970s thanks to the enterprising 'no-smoking' policy of the landlord. Since then it has been equally enterprising in its extensive range of beers from abroad.

Ordnance Survey column, Langerton Hill

From here turn right (away from the village) past Low Hall to locate an enclosed path leading down to the river. Turn right to follow the Wharfe upstream. When the river takes a big swing to the left, we are deflected right by an intervening wall to enter the farmyard at Woodhouse. Woodhouse is a 17th century manor house. Here we meet Barben Beck again just prior to its entry into the Wharfe. **When its access track turns right to join the road, go straight ahead to a footbridge and on again to a stile. The river is rejoined and soon leads back to Burnsall, omitting a final loop to cross the last field to a stile at the start of the bridge.**

St. Wilfred's, Burnsall

8

TROLLERS GILL

START   *Appletreewick*   *Grid ref. SE 053601*

DISTANCE *7½ miles*

ORDNANCE SURVEY MAPS
1:50,000
Landranger 98 - Wensleydale & Upper Wharfedale
*   99 - Northallerton & Ripon*
*   104 - Leeds, Bradford & Harrogate*
1:25,000
Outdoor Leisure 2 - Yorkshire Dales South/West

ACCESS *Start from the village centre. During the season a large meadow near the village centre provides car parking. Other than this, parking is limited. Appletreewick is served by Skipton-Bolton Abbey-Grassington buses and the seasonal Dalesbus.*

Exceptional river scenery precedes one of Craven's best limestone features.

S   Appletreewick has several claims to fame, even though many visitors may best remember its delightful name. Here are three halls and two inns in amongst a wonderful assortment of cottages. All stand on or about the narrow road wandering through the village, from three storeyed High Hall at the top - note the tiny St. John's church nearby - to Low Hall at the very bottom. Probably the oldest however is the curiously named Mock Beggar Hall, a fine little edifice that once went by the title of Monk's Hall.

Of the two hostelries, the *Craven Arms* takes its name from the family of William Craven, a Dick Whittington character who found his fortune in London, becoming Lord Mayor in 1611. Not forgetting his beginnings he became a worthy local benefactor, having Burnsall's grammar school and a number of bridges in the district built. The *New Inn*, meanwhile, achieved national fame in the 1970s thanks to the enterprising 'no-smoking' policy of the landlord. Since then it has been equally enterprising in its extensive range of beers from abroad.

Leave Appletreewick by heading west out of the village on the Burnsall road, past the two inns and Low Hall to reach a walled path leading down to the Wharfe. Turn left alongside the river, though almost immediately deflected away from it, albeit briefly, through a succession of gates. On regaining the riverbank it is now clung to faithfully, through a couple of pastures before entering a delightfully wooded section. At its far end note the simple but touching memorial plate set into a rock. **Emerging into a field, forsake the river by bearing left to join a track out onto a narrow road at a bridge.**

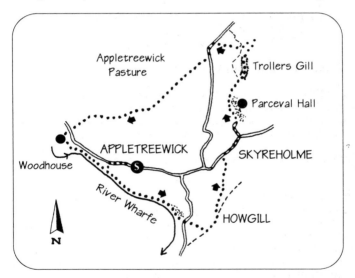

Cross the bridge and leave the road in favour of an enclosed track up to the left. At the top a rough lane is joined alongside the farm at Howgill: turn left along it past the caravan site at Howgill Lodge. Refreshments are normally available here. **A little beyond a barn look out for an old milestone set into the wall.** It points the way to

'Patley Bridge 6', indicating the former importance of Howgill Lane. **At this point go through a gate opposite and head away alongside the wall, first on its right, then its left. After a gateway slope down the field to a stile in the next wall, and continue down to cross a tiny beck behind which is another stile. Remain close to the main beck on the left now to soon arrive at a footbridge. Cross it and rise through a housing development to emerge onto the road at Skyreholme.**

Turn right along this quiet road, forking left at a bridge to the road end at the entrance to the grounds of Parceval Hall. The grandest house in upper Wharfedale was built over 300 years ago: its beautiful stonework looks out across Skyreholme to Simon's Seat, which totally dominates this corner of the valley. Now used as a diocesan retreat centre, the gardens and intermingled woodland are open to the public from Easter to October (small fee payable).

Take the gate just before the wooden bridge to follow Skyreholme Beck upstream on a good path. In a colourful enclosure the grass covered retaining wall of a reservoir is unmistakable. It was made to serve the mills of Skyreholme: now both dam and mills are history. **The path forks in the amphitheatre in front of Trollers Gill. The high wedge of Middle Hill divides the gorge from its parallel valley to the left: it is through this deep side valley with its old lead mining site that the public footpath continues after a look at Trollers Gill, for its inviting entrance just across to the right is not on a definitive right of way. However, as long as it is remains accessible under the Countryside Stewardship scheme, then bear right to reach its entrance, guarded by springs.**

Trollers Gill is a magnificent limestone gorge, often known as the 'Gordale of Wharfedale'. Though not particularly tall, the cliffs remain virtually unbroken for some distance. The narrow passage between is usually dry and safe, though it is renowned as the home of the legendary *Barguest*, a spectral hound with eyes like saucers!

*Simon's Seat
from the Wharfe
at Appletreewick*

At the far end of the ravine a ladder-stile sends the path on through more open country in the pleasant company of tiny Skyreholme Beck. Just after another stile, the beck is re-crossed to a stile over the adjacent wall. Here a thin path surmounts the gentle brow to run quickly on to rejoin the old mine track that runs around the west side of Middle Hill. Back on the public footpath bear right, briefly, and when it makes a sharp turn right, leave it by continuing straight ahead past the deep pothole of Hell Hole. Skirting a marshy area, swing left to approach the wall in front, soon reaching a stile onto the back road from Appletreewick up to the Pateley Bridge road.

Trollers Gill

Follow this road to the left, and a little beyond a bend take a gate on the right. A stony track crosses the broad upland of Appletreewick Pasture. The extensive panorama includes, clockwise, Barden Moor, the Malhamdale hills, Old Cote Moor, Grassington Moor, Great Whernside and Simon's Seat. Further along, a more intimate picture of the river's environs is revealed. Eventually the track drops gently down through two stiles by gates to the bottom corner of a field. Here leave the track in favour of a gate across to the right, from where a short walled section leads down to a crossroads of paths.

Unless time is pressing ignore the Appletreewick sign and take the gate directly ahead to run alongside a wall to two prominent barns. Initially enclosed by walls a track runs along to the right, soon descending to join the Appletreewick-Burnsall road. Cross straight over and down the access track to Woodhouse Farm (a 17th century manor house), turning to the left between the buildings to then make a bee-line for the riverbank. All that now remains is to accompany the Wharfe downstream, to return fairly shortly to the enclosed path by which we gained the river at the start of the walk. Retrace those early steps to therefore conclude the jaunt.

9

PENYGHENT GILL

START Litton   Grid ref. SD 905741

DISTANCE 8 miles

ORDNANCE SURVEY MAPS
1:50,000
Landranger 98 - Wensleydale & Upper Wharfedale
1:25,000
Outdoor Leisure 30 - Yorkshire Dales North/Central

ACCESS Start from the vicinity of the inn. There is roadside parking either here or further along the road in the village centre.

A fine circuit of a lively beck, and a superb green road.

S Litton is only the second largest village in the valley of the Skirfare, but has given its name to the valley once known as Amerdale. Its attractive buildings are strung along the road from the homely *Queens Arms*. Rising immediately behind and seen to good advantage on the return leg is Birks Fell, at 2001ft long regarded as the most innocuous of all Yorkshire's mountains. Recent mapping has now demoted it below the magical contour: the highest point is an imperceptible rise on a ridge stretching over 11 miles from Knipe Scar in the east to an arbitrary conclusion in Ribblesdale, beyond the wilds of Cosh.

From the pub head west through the village and leave the road just beyond the telephone box, down a drive to the left immediately before two barns usher the road out of Litton. Bear left of a short wall to a narrow wooden footbridge across the river Skirfare, then head for a gap-stile just to the right. Two fields are then crossed diagonally to a pair of barns in the corner of the second. From a gate by the main barn turn right to join an enclosed track, which is then followed along to the right to arrive alongside New Bridge.

Without crossing the bridge keep straight on to a gate in front, from where a rough track climbs the hillside. This is to be our return route, but for now make use of only a few yards of it then break off across the field to locate a small gate in the wall ahead. After the next field a pleasant walled section returns us to the water's edge, though it is no longer the Skirfare but Hesleden Beck just short of its confluence with the river. As Nether Heselden is approached a bridge conveys us over the beck, then turn sharp left through a gate onto the access road to the farm. Nether Heselden is an ancient settlement in a surround of greenery, and is the only habitation between Litton and Halton Gill.

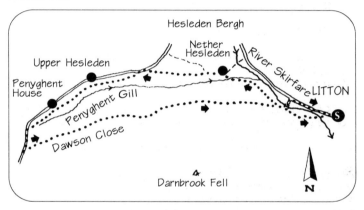

Keep left to pass between the buildings to a gate from where a track climbs to another gate. From the adjacent stile a narrow trod accompanies a fence as it rises unceasingly above the beck. Part way up Penyghent appears, soon followed by Fountains Fell up to the left, above our return route. A major feature of the walk is the extended opportunity to survey Penyghent from a lesser known angle. At 2273ft this crouching lion oversees more than half of the walk.

Eventually the fence swings sharp right to join the fell road out of Halton Gill. Turn left along it as far as the first cattle-grid (a matter of yards), and beyond it turn down to a gate in the wall below. Drop a little further and then turn right on an increasingly clear trod, parallel with the gill throughout a splendid length beneath Upper Hesleden.

Eventually the enclosures below Penyghent House are skirted to arrive at a mini-ravine beneath a cave entrance. Just beneath us, Penyghent Gill is a lovely beck, but like much of today's water it is often under the ground. **On entering a larger pasture maintain the same course, closing in on the head of the gill and crossing a rocky tributary to arrive at a gate back onto the road.** A grassy mound in the penultimate enclosure is an ancient burial mound known as the Giant's Grave. **Turn left again for just a few more minutes to reach a guidepost identifying a bridle road doubling back across Dawson Close to Litton.**

Penyghent from Penyghent Gill

This outstanding example of a green road has like many packhorse routes escaped being surfaced, to remain as one of the most distinguishable features of the Yorkshire Dales. Evidence of its road status can be found on signposts at either end. Where it meets the valley road beyond New Bridge a forlorn roadsign of not-too-distant origin points the seven miles to Stainforth. Needless to say it provides some splendid views, firstly to Halton Gill and the head of Littondale, and later down to Litton and beyond. **With full steam ahead it transports us unerringly back to New Bridge, and the opening half-mile or the quiet road then lead equally clearly back to the village.**

10

MOOR END

START *Kettlewell*   *Grid ref. SD 968722*

DISTANCE *5 miles*

ORDNANCE SURVEY MAPS
1:50,000
Landranger 98 - Wensleydale & Upper Wharfedale
1:25,000
Outdoor Leisure 30 - Yorkshire Dales North/Central

ACCESS *Start from the village centre. There is a large car park at the entrance. Kettlewell is served by occasional buses from Skipton via Grassington, and by seasonal Dalesbus.*

After an early climb this is an easy walk encircling the river and giving fine views both up and down the valley. On each leg of the walk the other half can easily be surveyed across the dale. Unlike the outward leg, the return calls for no effort other than the stamina needed to surmount the ladder-stiles.

S Kettlewell is the hub of the upper dale, a junction of roads and natural halting place. It stands on what was a major coaching route to Richmond, and the two inns at the entrance to the village would have serviced the weary travellers. The route in question is now a surfaced road, but still provides a tortuous way over Park Rash and into Coverdale. Shops, tearooms a third inn and plentiful accommodation - including a youth hostel - add more life to a village being steadily engulfed by holiday homes.

Kettlewell straddles its own beck which largely drains the slopes of Great Whernside, very much Kettlewell's mountain. These slopes bear the scars of lead mining, the one-time industry now replaced by tourism as a partner to farming. Some delectable cottages and gardens

43

line the beck as it races through the village. Footpaths positively radiate from Kettlewell to all points of the compass, and one could spend a richly-varied holiday week here without the need of any transport. Just set off in a new direction!

Leave Kettlewell by crossing the main bridge at the southern entrance to the village, then forsake the road for the higher of two gates on the right. From it a good level path heads away, ignoring the Arncliffe branch which starts an early climb to the prominent 'Slit'. Our track remains on the wall-side: after a level section it bears left in front of a clump of trees, crosses a tiny beck and then commences to zigzag up the hillside. In no time at all it resumes its level course to run pleasantly along to Moor End.

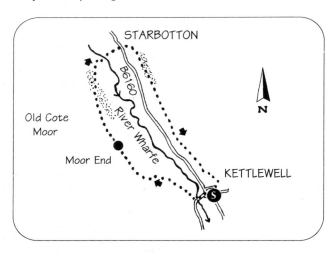

This second mile of the walk centred on Moor End is a near level trek at around the 1200ft contour, and affords a simply glorious panorama of Upper Wharfedale. The villages of Buckden, Starbotton and Kettlewell are dwarfed by the immense bulk of three 2000-footers rising beyond the meandering Wharfe. The central feature, Buckden Pike, exhibits various lead mining remains on its slopes. The fell is flanked by Great Whernside to its south and Yockenthwaite Moor to its north. A former sheep farm turned outdoor education centre, isolated Moor End is the highest point of the walk.

Enter the yard and turn left with the wall rising away. Through the corner gate leave the green track rising away, and continue along the wall-top to a gap-stile in it. Cross the field, through a collapsed wall and on with a wall on the right to a corner stile. On a little further the Arncliffe-Starbotton bridleway is joined at a gate.

Turn through the bridle-gate to earn an exhilarating arrival atop a steep drop to the valley. The way slants gently away from the wall before commencing a steeper, sunken drop into an old wood. It slants all the way down, emerging at the bottom between hoary, lichen-covered walls. By a barn at the bottom it swings right to a footbridge over the Wharfe, a track then leading up to the road in Starbotton.

Situated midway between the better known villages of Kettlewell and Buckden, tiny Starbotton witnesses all that passes through the dale, even though only a small number pause here. The usual reason for halting is to visit the attractive, whitewashed *Fox & Hounds*. Off the main road are some lovely corners with 17th century cottages, including a 1665 datestone opposite the pub. Starbotton nestles beneath the slopes of Buckden Pike, and like its neighbours stands away from the river on its own swift-flowing beck. Cam Gill Beck cuts a deep groove in the flank of the pike, and in 1686 was swollen by a deluge which caused disastrous flooding in the village.

Walk a yard or two to the right from the point of entry onto the road, and turn up the lane opposite. Use a gate on the right to commence the return to Kettlewell. Follow a track up through three small pastures to enter one with a barn in it, then take a gate just to its left. Now turn right alongside the wall to begin a long, easy march through innumerable pastures, punctuated by a succession of stiles in intervening walls. Throughout its course the path remains virtually level and clear, with a line of unsightly telegraph poles playing their part in pointing the way.

When Kettlewell finally appears just ahead the path descends a little towards it, and the village is entered by a turn down to the right to a stile onto a short-lived enclosed path. This debouches onto a back road in the village: turn right for the quickest way back onto the main road through Kettlewell.

11

BOLTON ABBEY

START *Bolton Abbey*   *Grid ref. SE 077552*

DISTANCE *4½ miles*

ORDNANCE SURVEY MAPS
1:50,000
Landranger 104 - Leeds, Bradford & Harrogate
1:25,000
Outdoor Leisure 2 - Yorkshire Dales South/West

ACCESS *Start from the Cavendish Pavilion, signposted off the B6160 just north of Bolton Abbey, turning off by the large memorial fountain. There is a large car park. The B6265 is served by Skipton-Bolton Abbey-Grassington buses and by the seasonal Dalesbus.*

A simple riverside stroll on good paths in splendid surroundings. The central feature, in sight for much of the walk, is the hoary old ruin of Upper Wharfedale's most famous building. Alternative starts are Bolton Bridge and Bolton Abbey village.

❺ **From the Cavendish Pavilion set off back along the drive, but from the gate by the cattle-grid go left into the car park and follow an access track along the bank of the Wharfe. When the track ends keep company with the river until the pasture itself abruptly ends, then climb to a stile to emerge onto the road at the Cavendish Memorial Fountain.** This commemorates Lord Frederick Cavendish, who was murdered in Phoenix Park, Dublin in 1882. **Turn left for only a couple of minutes to a gate into the priory grounds. The most direct route back towards the river is down through the graveyard, but surely few will not halt to explore the ruins and the priory church.**

46

Bolton Abbey is, strictly, the name for the tiny village whose show-piece is more correctly the priory. The imposing ruin forms a magnet for close-at-hand West Yorkshire visitors, with the river hereabouts being an attraction in its own right. The priory dates from 1154 and was built by Augustinian canons who moved here from nearby Embsay. At the Dissolution the nave was spared, and remains to this day the parish church. There is much else of interest in the vicinity, including adjacent Bolton Hall dating from the 17th century, a large and splendid example of a tithe barn, an antiquarian bookshop, a Post office/shop and various refreshments. The village car park would in fact make a useful alternative starting point, the first sighting of the priory then being the classic framed view through the 'Hole in the Wall'.

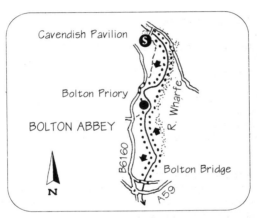

On arriving at the wooden bridge and its adjacent stepping stones do not be tempted to cross, but instead follow the river downstream again. A long, pleasant pasture leads all the way to Bolton Bridge, the river being crossed by a footbridge in its shadow.

At Bolton Bridge the large hotel bears the arms of the Duke of Devonshire, hardly surprising as almost everything here still belongs to that estate. Across the road is a cafe. The shapely bridge loses a little grandeur due to its adjacent modern footbridge, but still marks the Wharfe's departure from the National Park. 1994 saw the completion of the Bolton Bridge by-pass, which now leaves the old crossing in peace.

Bolton Bridge

Within yards turn left along an enclosed way between a cottage and Red Lion Farm, to enter a riverside pasture. As the Wharfe is neared we are deflected around a steep, wooded bank, then drop back down to cross three pastures, parallel with the nearby Wharfe. After a tiny beck and a stile a field is climbed, remaining with the left-hand fence to a stile and a superb high-level vantage point.

From the stile a good path runs along to the right, being joined by another as it heads through the trees a fair way above the river. The path ends on meeting a narrow road as it prepares to ford Pickles Beck: a footbridge caters for dry-shod pedestrians. On the other side a stile gives access to the riverbank for the final few minutes back to the pavilion bridge.

Tithe Barn,
Bolton Abbey

12

UPPER LITTONDALE

START *Halton Gill*   *Grid ref. SD 880764*

DISTANCE *5½ miles*

ORDNANCE SURVEY MAPS
1:50,000
Landranger 98 - Wensleydale & Upper Wharfedale
1:25,000
Outdoor Leisure 2 - Yorkshire Dales South/West **or**
Outdoor Leisure 30 - Yorkshire Dales North/Central

ACCESS *Start in the centre of the hamlet. There is reasonable parking, notably the lay-by opposite the green.*

Easy walking, with good beck scenery in typically bleak Pennine surroundings.

S Halton Gill is the first sizeable settlement in Littondale. Its cluster of grey buildings include a centuries-old chapel and even a grammar school, but both now serve as private dwellings. **From the junction by the green turn down the Stainforth road and over the bridge, then leave by a stile on the right to descend to the riverbank.**

Now accompany the Skirfare upstream, taking in several gates and stiles before a new path squeezes between pens and river to emerge onto the road at Foxup Bridge. Turn right over the said structure and immediately left on a broad track. Early on we pass a charming scene where a tiny arched bridge spans the lively beck as it tumbles over limestone ledges. **The rough farm road heads unerringly up the valley, gradually rising above Cosh Beck to eventually arrive at Cosh, the first building since Foxup.**

Cosh is Remote: geographically it stands at the very heart of the National Park, but it couldn't be further from the centre of things! A thriving farmstead earlier this century, it spent many unoccupied years, though it has now undergone restoration. Interestingly, Littondale's highest building is only a five mile walk from Horton-in-Ribblesdale's railway station, a trek undertaken by its former occupants. The name Cosh is of Norse origin, and was also at one time a grange of Fountains Abbey.

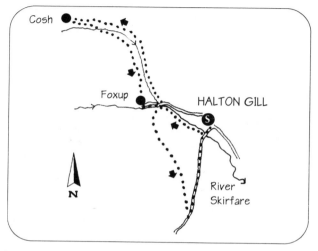

Without entering the confines of Cosh, turn off the track to commence the return journey by descending towards the beck, but only as far as the brink of the steeper drop to the water's edge. Maintaining this level, head downstream as far as a sizeable sheepfold which was probably seen on the outward journey. At this point descend to the beck, fording it and continuing downstream to an immediately intervening wall. From the stile in it rise very slightly across the large pasture to locate a stile in the next wall.

From here on a series of stiles lead through pathless fields, virtually parallel with the beck below. Eventually Foxup appears ahead, and from a gateway descend a field to the nearest buildings. A stile and a gate between them give access to a track which drops down to Foxup Beck, crossing it to the road terminus and Foxup Bridge Farm.

Foxup is a farming hamlet marking the upper limit of the valley's surfaced road. At Foxup Bridge the two hitherto moorland becks combine to create the Skirfare. The walk's final couple of miles from here on provide grand views both down the dale and also across to Halton Gill nestling beneath Horse Head Moor.

Halton Gill in the depths of winter,
sheltering beneath Horse Head Moor

Do not continue to Foxup Bridge again, but take a gate opposite the farm and a track up the field. After a second gate the track bears across to a gate in the right-hand wall: do not use it but continue up the field, soon levelling out to arrive at a gate in the far left corner. Remaining level a large pasture is crossed to another gate, the path then running on through low outcrops of limestone to merge with the Stainforth road.

Turn left, preferably on the grassy verges for a straightforward descent into Halton Gill, a clear target in the valley bottom. The Skirfare is crossed for the last time to conclude the walk.

13

HEBDEN GILL

START *Hebden*   *Grid ref. SE 026631*

DISTANCE *3½ miles*

ORDNANCE SURVEY MAPS
1:50,000
Landranger 98 - Wensleydale & Upper Wharfedale
1:25,000
Outdoor Leisure 2 - Yorkshire Dales South/West

ACCESS *Start at the top end of the village, where the main street joins the B6265 Grassington-Pateley Bridge road. There is roadside parking. Served by bus from Skipton via Grassington.*

A fascinating glimpse into the past, both ancient and relatively recent. A gentle stroll with just one slightly rough section.

S Hebden is a small village on the Pateley Bridge road. North of the road where our walk starts is Town Hill, the top end of the village. Here is a photogenic grouping of cottages and an old bridge, while just up the hill is the village pub, the *Clarendon*. The bulk of Hebden stands below the road, including the church which when built saved the parishioners the walk to Linton. The Wharfe is a long way below the village, and is crossed by a suspension footbridge. Hebden, like its bigger neighbour Grassington, grew with the once thriving lead mining industry, with Hebden Gill, and above it Grassington Moor, abounding in evocative reminders of those hard days.

From Town Hill crossroads below the pub, take the traffic-free road up the side of the beck. Already the surroundings are delightful: our return route comes back over that edge high up to the right. **Remain on the road for about three-quarters of a mile until its demise at the hamlet of Hole Bottom.**

The lane is replaced by a good track which forks right through a gate to drop down to cross a small bridge over Hebden Beck. This former miners' track now accompanies the sparkling beck upstream. Rising gently alongside the beck, evidence of the lead mining industry appears and an area of spoil heaps and ruinous buildings is entered.

A little beyond the site of a tiny reservoir on the right, the main track drops down to ford the beck before inflowing Bolton Gill joins it. This is the turning point of the walk, so without crossing either beck, turn up a beckoning path up the slope to the right. Looking up the deep cleft of this side valley, a dark shadow will be seen near the top. It is a former winding shaft from around 1856, and restored by the Earby Mines Research Group.

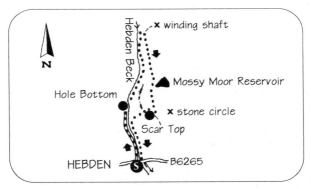

Our return route, however, forsakes the inviting path at the first opportunity, in favour of a path which curves back up to the right through the bracken. It is narrow but easy to follow, passing an old mine level before reaching a gate. On this contouring section there are increasingly good views over to Barden Moor, with the Cracoe Fell obelisk prominent. Behind us, meanwhile, the upper reaches of Hebden Gill merge into Grassington Moor, with a restored smelt mill chimney in evidence (see WALK 29).

The gate admits to an area of rough pasture, and a sketchy path maintains a near level trod through this and two further pastures, finding the exit from the third by being deflected left of a ruinous section of wall. This last section detours around a collapsed mineshaft that has been fenced off for our and the sheep's protection.

From the gate the path continues by the right-hand wall to the next gate ahead. Tempting here is a short detour to the conspicuous level outline to the left. It is the retaining wall of Mossy Moor Reservoir, at a breezy thousand feet up, another relic from mining days. When traversed to the right, its little embankment points back to the path. **From the gate ahead open moorland is reached, and a good track skirts the sea of heather as we continue by the wall.**

The route turns off where the wall turns sharp right to accommodate the access road to Scar Top House. At this point a short section of collapsed wall strikes away towards a stone circle, 150 yards distant and almost lost in dense heather. Mossy Moor's modest stone circle consists of four major stones, and eight in total. **At the wall corner, meanwhile, turn to follow the track in towards Scar Top House. Note that a wall-stile beyond the cattle-grid marks the actual right of way.**

Do not enter the private yard of the house but follow its enclosing wall around to the right to arrive at a gateway and gap-stile, immediately beneath which is a sudden drop back into Hebden Gill. The dramatic view includes the bulk of Burnsall Fell and the distant outline of Pendle Hill: a superb moment, with the tangle of boulders of Care Scar just to the right. **A short, steep section ensues as a thin path turns down the wall-side, and a green zigzag works down to a gate below. A faint green path heads over the brow, going left to the wall and curving down with it to a corner stile at the end. Head on to one at the next corner and slant down a faint green way to rejoin Hebden Beck.**

From a stile there either cross the footbridge to the road on which we began, or preferably remain on this bank down to a row of cottages and thence the road bridge in Hebden.

Winding shaft,
Bolton Gill

14

STRID WOOD

START Bolton Abbey   Grid ref. SE 077552

DISTANCE 6½ miles

ORDNANCE SURVEY MAPS
1:50,000
Landranger 104 - Leeds, Bradford & Harrogate
1:25,000
Outdoor Leisure 2 - Yorkshire Dales South/West

ACCESS Start from the Cavendish Pavilion, signposted off the B6160 just north of Bolton Abbey, turning by the large memorial fountain. There is a large car park. The B6160 is served by Skipton-Bolton Abbey-Grassington buses, and by seasonal services including Dalesbus.

An outstanding juxtaposition of river and woodland, and an absolute riot of autumn colour.

S This delectable section of the Wharfe is part of the Duke of Devonshire's Bolton Abbey estate, and a combination of largely permissive paths allows good access to both banks. Paths along the west bank have been incorporated into nature trails, and a leaflet available at the shop helps to unravel the colour codes. With the exception of the Pavilion to Posforth Bridge all the paths remain private, though *'the public are invited to walk and picnic'* in a manner that captures the Victorian flavour still evident in some of the quainter touches hereabouts. The Pavilion itself has seen major improvements in recent years, and offers all kinds of refreshments.

Other than at the Strid, it is the woodland that steals the show from the river. Strid Wood is a hugely popular riverside habitat where man and nature appear to co-exist with little difficulty. The importance of the woodland for bird and plant life has been recognised by designation as a Site of Special Scientific Interest (SSSI) and this should be respected by keeping to the paths. This should not pose any problems, for a splendid network was laid out during the 19th century, being well maintained ever since.

From the pavilion cross the wooden bridge and turn upstream. Shortly after entering woods the path runs to Posforth Gill Bridge, but avoids the road by a new footbridge to remain in the woods. It clings to the river until presented with a fork, where a simple choice is complicated by the respective attractions of either branch. The lower path is at times an exciting clamber over water-washed rocks, and caution is needed if the river is high: the path runs past the Strid to eventually meet the higher path.

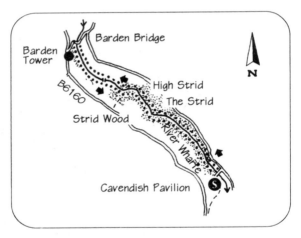

Firmly recommended is the higher level option, despite its surprisingly sustained pull to the top of the wood. Hereafter easy walking ensues along a magnificent terrace. Although a couple of paths later break off down to the river, the only point of any possible doubt occurs just after the climb, keeping left at a crossroads to pass a resthouse. Bedecked with a luxuriant bilberry thatch, the up-market rest house is sited at the first of many well-chosen viewpoints on the high path. One particular glimpse gives a surprise cameo of the Strid, perfectly framed by foliage. Shortly afterwards comes another classic, as the High Strid is revealed in a contrastingly open setting. **On re-uniting, the path leaves the wood to run past a sturdy aqueduct to arrive at Barden Bridge.**

Those with time to spare will enjoy a detour up the road after crossing the bridge, for just two minutes above are the ruins of Barden Tower. This was built as a hunting lodge by the Cliffords of Skipton Castle, and boasted two famous residents from that family. Henry the 'Shepherd' Lord came in 1485, being raised in the Cumbrian fells until the end of the Wars of the Roses. Up to his death in 1523 he preferred Barden's peace and the company of the canons of Bolton to the splendour of Skipton. He also had the adjacent chapel built. The indomitable Lady Anne had the tower restored in 1659 and spent much of her final years here, a stone tablet on an exterior wall surviving to confirm her work. In 1676 she died, last of the Cliffords, and the long process of decay began.

Back at the bridge a stile kicks off the return leg, soon emerging from trees for another grassy spell past the aqueduct. On entering Strid Wood a network of nature trail paths give a colourful choice, though the main path is obvious throughout. An early detour stays nearest the river to savour the High Strid and a rock pinnacle - the Hawkstone - above the rocky path. Either way the Strid itself, further downstream, cannot be missed. Here is the focal point of the wood, as the Wharfe is forced through a narrow gritstone channel of great depth. Lives have been lost here in senseless attempts to leap the foaming waters. Many decades ago visitors could travel here in style, by wagonette from the old railway station. **The broad carriageway now leads gently back to the Cavendish Pavilion.**

The Strid

15

THORPE FELL TOP

START Linton   Grid. ref. SD 997627

DISTANCE 9 miles

ORDNANCE SURVEY MAPS
1;50,000
Landranger 98 - Wensleydale & Upper Wharfedale
                103 - Blackburn & Burnley
                104 - Leeds, Bradford & Harrogate
1;25,000
Outdoor Leisure 2 - Yorkshire Dales South/West

ACCESS Park in the village centre, either by the green or on the
road through the village. Served by Skipton-Grassington bus.

A fine stretch of moorland rambling, contrasting well with the tiny
villages under the steep slopes.

• *IMPORTANT* The moorland section of this walk is part of the Duke
of Devonshire's estate. Between the fell lanes out of Thorpe and
Cracoe we are on access land which may be closed on certain days
during the grouse shooting season (not Sundays) and at times of high
fire risk. Notices are posted at the access points, but for advance
information, contact Grassington National Park Centre or the estate
office. Dogs are not allowed on the access area.

S   Linton is generally accepted as being one of northern England's
most attractive villages, and not without good reason. A rich assortment of limestone buildings stand in very laid-back fashion, none
wishing to crowd the spacious green. Nearest is the whitewashed little
hostelry, whose name recalls a local benefactor. Richard Fountaine
made his money in London, but in his will he remembered Linton by

paying for the 'hospital' at the end of the green. This 18th century building remains in use as almshouses. Through the green runs Linton Beck, crossed in quick succession by a road bridge, a ford, a clapper bridge and most strikingly, a packhorse bridge.

From the *Fountaine Inn* cross the green and the beck and follow the lane right to its imminent demise at a farm. Turn left in front of a large barn and along a briefly enclosed track. At the end it climbs with the left-hand wall, and though it peters out remain with the wall to negotiate three intervening stiles. From the third head away in the same direction, rising through a large field and going left of a line of trees to a ruinous barn. A stile to its left admits onto roughly surfaced Thorpe Lane. Turn left to follow its narrow course into Thorpe.

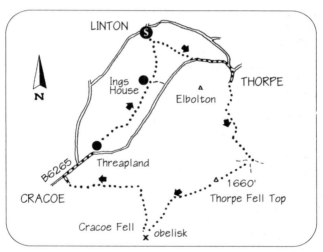

The farming hamlet of Thorpe is known for its elusiveness which allegedly kept it hidden from the marauding Scots. Romantically titled Thorpe in the Hollow it shelters between reef knolls and below the overpowering Thorpe Fell. Note the triangular little enclosed green. Most prominent in the Linton and Thorpe scene are the rounded hills known as reef knolls. Of limestone with a grass covering, they are relics of underwater mounds, since exposed by the eventual erosion of overlying rocks. Immediately west of Thorpe is Elbolton, probably the best example.

Bear right at the triangular junction in the centre and keep on until the road dissolves into a couple of rough tracks. Opt for the left one which climbs steeply between walls to emerge at an access point onto the open moor. Two sunken tracks head directly away from the gate, and it is the right-hand one which is to be preferred. It swings up to the right to terminate at the remains of a small quarry. Here turn up to the left in a southerly direction, a track reappearing at a cairn. On rounding the beginnings of a beck the track regains its groove, though loses it briefly again at a faint fork. Keep right to rise up a gentle slope, and as the groove disappears for good a stone shooting house appears ahead, and is soon reached.

At the shooting house our track ends, but a wider track encountered is of little use to us. Though it can be followed a short distance to the right, it must then be forsaken in order to climb the modest slope directly behind the building. Though pathless, a short half-mile will lead to the Ordnance Survey column (S5312) on Thorpe Fell Top.

At 1660ft, Thorpe Fell Top is the infrequently visited summit of Barden Moor. This huge mass is contained in a triangle bounded by the Skipton-Threshfield-Bolton Abbey roads, and consists of a pudding-like tract of heather moorland. This unashamedly gritstone landscape contrasts markedly with the limestone country at the start of the walk. Though outcropping on the summit, the boulders are most profuse where they line the rim of the plateau in typical gritstone edge fashion.

*Approaching
the obelisk
on Cracoe Fell*

The view from the summit is a splendid all-round panorama, though devoid of any immediate interest. Some of the principal features are listed (clockwise from east):- Simon's Seat; Earl Seat; Beamsley Beacon; Rombald's Moor; Chelker Reservoir; Skipton Moor; Oxenhope Moor; Boulsworth Hill; Pendle Hill; Bowland moors; Malhamdale hills; Ingleborough; Fountains Fell; Birks Fell; Kilnsey Crag; Yockenthwaite Moor; Buckden Pike; Great Whernside; Grimwith Reservoir; Greenhow Hill.

After admiring the view it is necessary to engage in a further bout of heather bashing by aiming in a south-westerly direction for the conspicuous obelisk on Cracoe Fell. An inscribed boundary stone is met just short of the depression between the felltop and the monument. It divides Cracoe and Thorpe parishes, and its 'B' side is inscribed 'DD', yet more evidence of ownership. **Here swing right in front of a row of grouse butts to join the substantial wall along the crest of the escarpment. Now turn left on a path by the wall for an easy walk up to the monument, a stile provides access to it.**

Cracoe's memorial to its war dead is a major Wharfedale landmark. The solid structure is made of the same rock on which it is perched, and not surprisingly it commands a glorious view. Its moor-edge location ensures that distant Dales mountains are complemented by a rich collection of villages such as Hetton, Threshfield and Grassington.

Next objective is the head of Fell Lane climbing out of Cracoe. It is seen just to the right of the village, and just to the right of a stream at the foot of the moor. While one could make a direct descent, engaging, for a while, a sunken way directly beneath us, there is a far more useful old way to be found. Head along the slope from the obelisk, in line with the wall over to the right, a faint trod forming: this meets the sunken way starting to go down beneath the monument. Cross straight over to find another winding down, on a bend. Turn down it past a basic stone shelter, the way unmistakable now as it slants down the fell.

The innumerable braided ways here are old sledgates, worn deep by the passage of sledges loaded with quarried stone, and long since grassed over. This great groove absorbs several other such tracks, leaving the rougher slopes then eventually doubling back to falter in the reedy ground before the bottom wall. The intake gate is just along to the left, defended by sheep pens. At this point we depart the access

61

area. The lane is a splendid green way itself in its first half, before the addition of a farm track makes it more standard. **At a cottage it becomes surfaced, to join the main road. The *Devonshire Arms* is just yards along to the left.**

The little settlement of Cracoe marks the barely discernible watershed between Airedale and Wharfedale. Its long, low white-walled inn has a good few years' history behind it and like several others in the vicinity it bears the arms of the family on whose moor we have just been tramping. There is also a very popular cafe just along the street.

Turn right along the busy road and leave it at the first opportunity along a pleasanter back road. This too is left at the first chance in favour of a short track to Threapland Farm on the left. After crossing the beck turn right in front of the main buildings to a gate from where an initially enclosed track heads away. On departing the environs of Threapland, one's eyes cannot fail to be drawn by the scene of utter devastation presented by the quarry to the left. **When faced by a fence the track forks, and our now pathless course follows the fence around to the right to a stile. From the tiny beck behind it aim directly across two fields, then bear a little to the left above a small wood to locate the next stile.**

Two narrow fields are crossed to descend the next one to a tiny beck and Ings House's access road in front of a barn. Cross them both to a stile just left of the barn, and from the next stile follow the right-hand wall across a larger field. From the gate at the end a tractor track leads across the final field to rejoin the track by which we left Linton. Turn left to re-enter the village and end the walk.

At Linton

16

GREAT WHERNSIDE

START Kettlewell   Grid ref. SD 968722

DISTANCE 6 miles

ORDNANCE SURVEY MAPS
1:50,000
Landranger 98 - Wensleydale & Upper Wharfedale
1:25,000
Outdoor Leisure 30 - Yorkshire Dales North/Central

ACCESS Start from the village centre. There is a large car park at the entrance. Kettlewell is served by occasional buses from Skipton via Grassington and also by seasonal services.

A charming beckside ramble precedes a short and easy fellwalk to Wharfedale's highest top.

S Kettlewell is the hub of the upper dale, a junction of roads and natural halting place. It stands on what was a major coaching route to Richmond, and the two inns at the entrance to the village would have serviced the weary travellers. The route in question is now a surfaced road, but still provides a tortuous way over Park Rash and into Coverdale. Shops, tearooms a third inn and plentiful accommodation - including a youth hostel - add more life to a village being steadily engulfed by holiday homes.

Kettlewell straddles its own beck which largely drains the slopes of Great Whernside, very much Kettlewell's mountain. These slopes bear the scars of lead mining, the one-time industry now replaced by tourism as a partner to farming. Some delectable cottages and gardens line the beck as it races through the village, while footpaths positively radiate from Kettlewell to all points of the compass.

From the car park head into the village and leave the main road immediately before the bridge by the two hotels, turning along the road to the right. Fork left at the maypole to pass the church, and at the *Kings Head* turn sharp right on a lane alongside the beck. At a shapely bridge and chapel the lane becomes a track, and just a little further it crosses Dowber Gill Beck: here leave it by turning up the little beckside path to a gate in the adjacent wall. Now turn right to begin a long mile and a quarter keeping very close company with the beck.

Several stiles and some waterfalls are encountered and little height gained until the unmistakable site of Providence Pot is reached, crossing the beck just before it. Providence Pot is one of the Dales' better known potholes, and is well sited in the centre of the beck. An incongruous manhole cover guards the vertical entrance. The slopes above are scarred with the remnants of old lead workings.

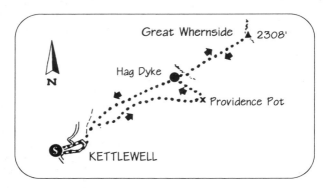

Directly behind is the meeting of twin becks, but our path is the very clear one up the left-hand slope immediately next to the pothole. Re-cross the beck and climb the path (not currently recorded as a definitive right of way) which soon levels out to approach Hag Dyke. At 1525ft, Hag Dyke is one of the highest buildings in the country. It is now put to use as a scouts' outdoor centre. Do not enter its confines but climb the wide path up the steep scarp to a line of cairns at the top. The summit now appears directly ahead, and the path crosses a damp plateau before a steady climb to the highest point. This final mile to the summit, in regular use since time immemorial, has only recently been designated as a definitive right of way.

Great Whernside is not only the highest of Wharfedale's fells, it is by far the bulkiest. Only from Kettlewell is there anything like easy access. To the east innumerable square miles of bleak moorland fall to the upper reaches of Nidderdale, indeed the Nidd is born within a mile of the summit. Atop the line of Long Crags - large 'scrambling' boulders - stands an Ordnance Survey column (2976) at 2308ft, and an immense pile of stones, a real cairn and a half. The National Park boundary runs along this summit ridge.

The view is largely one of fells, from the nearby mass of Buckden Pike to the distant Three Peaks, of which Penyghent looks particularly distinguished. A short but lovely section of Wharfedale can be seen from Kilnsey Crag to Grass Wood.

To return to Kettlewell retrace steps to Hag Dyke and enter its yard by a gate by some sheep pens just beyond the building. Follow the access track out to a gate, then leave it to drop half-left to eventually meet a left hand wall. Keep parallel with the beck far below, and a sketchy path works its way back to the track over Dowber Gill Beck. The finish can be varied by crossing the bridge by the chapel.

Hag Dyke

17

BARDEN MOOR

START Barden   Grid ref. SE 052573

DISTANCE 8 miles

ORDNANCE SURVEY MAPS
1:50,000
Landranger 104 - Leeds, Bradford & Harrogate
1:25,000
Outdoor Leisure 2 - Yorkshire Dales South/West

ACCESS Start from the sizeable riverside parking area at Barden
Bridge. In the season the adjacent field is opened up. Barden, just
up the hill, is served by Skipton-Bolton Abbey-Grassington buses.

Easy walking through a rich moorland tapestry, topped off with a
riverbank saunter.

NOTE BEFORE STARTING The walk crosses the Wharfe by stepping
stones at Drebley, a potential impasse if the river is high or one's
confidence is low. They are, however, in good condition.

•IMPORTANT The entire moorland section of the walk is on access
land which may be closed on certain days during the grouse shooting
season (not Sundays) and at times of high fire risk. Notices are posted
at all the access points, but for advance information, contact either
Grassington National Park Centre or the estate office. It is worth noting
that dogs are not allowed on the access area.

S Barden Moor is a special tract of upland, a vast playground both
for the thoughtful rambler and the less unobtrusive 'sportsman'.
Above the intake walls encircling the moor, bracken flanks give way
to heather and rough grass, where one can follow paths and tracks or

simply roam free. The success of the access arrangement here must be anathema to the greedy landowners elsewhere who attempt to deny us our heritage; certainly the sheep and the nesting birds appear unperturbed, though the grouse do tend to get restless when August approaches. The millstone grit outcrops and edges that characterise the northern and western scarps of the moor are absent from this walk, which instead explores the hinterland, in the heart of the moor.

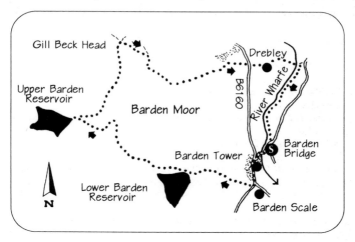

At Barden is the Wharfe's finest bridge. A tablet dates its restoration - 'at the charge of the whole West Riding' as 1676. **Start by crossing the bridge and up the road climbing steeply to Barden Tower.** Barden Tower was built as a hunting lodge by the powerful Cliffords of Skipton Castle, and it boasted two famous residents from that family. Henry the 'Shepherd' Lord came in 1485, being raised in the Cumbrian fells until the Wars of the Roses ended. Up to his death in 1523 he preferred Barden's peace and the company of the canons of Bolton to Skipton's splendour. He also had the adjacent chapel built.

The redoubtable Lady Anne had the Tower restored in 1659 and spent much of her final years here, a stone tablet on an exterior wall surviving to confirm her work. In 1676 she died, last of the Cliffords, and the long process of decay began. The beautifully maintained chapel is currently operating as a restaurant.

On leaving, turn left along the main road just as far as the Skipton turning. Only yards up it, escape by a gate on the right to enter the access area. A stony track heads off up the moor to the dam of Lower Barden Reservoir. The track runs on past its head (from the cattle-grid note the thatched shooting houses across the beck) before a climb to the dam of its higher neighbour. On the final pull the obelisk on Cracoe Fell (see WALK 15) is seen on the skyline ahead.

Colliery chimney, Gill Beck Head

After a potter about, return a few yards to a junction where a footpath sign to Burnsall invites a foot-friendlier ramble on a traditional moorland track. It maintains a near level course for some time, contouring splendidly round to an attractive little dam at Gill Beck Head. This is the jewelled tarn of Barden Moor's 'Lake District'. A delectable spot for a sandwich break, it is also a haunt of gulls. In view from it, just up the slope, is a chimney from a former colliery, worked to supply coal for the lead smelting mill on Grassington Moor. Stone was also quarried at various locations on the moor.

Across its modest embankment a crossroads is reached: at 1214ft this is the highest point of the walk. Turn right on a track through the heather, running along to join a similar track by some grouse butts. Once again going right, this one drops down to a crossroads by another row of butts. At this junction turn left, the broad track soon becoming delightful underfoot as it runs on towards the moor edge. The final grassy knoll is a good place to halt and take stock, with a

The chapel, Barden Tower

marvellous prospect across the valley to the deep bowl of the Appletreewick-Skyreholme area. **Below, the track drops down to the head of a green lane, at which point the access area is departed. The lane descends directly to the Burnsall road.**

Almost opposite, the access road to Drebley provides immediate escape as it resumes our fall to the river. Drebley itself is a timeless farming community that was once a forest lodge. **After the first building turn into the farmyard on the left, continuing straight through to emerge on a level, green track. It crosses a field, then part way through the next one turn down to a gateway at the very bottom. Below, the Wharfe's bank is gained at the stepping stones.**

Barden Tower

Drebley's stepping stones display much character: a refusal will incur three penalty points and more importantly retraced steps, for there is no path in either direction on Drebley's bank of the Wharfe. Those of a nervous disposition will find no solace in the knowledge that a footbridge existed here a number of decades ago. Upstream on the east bank is a barn that was formerly Hough Mill, restored by none other than Lady Anne Clifford, in 1657.

Moving swiftly (on paper, at least) to the opposite bank the final stage of the walk traces a very beautiful and tranquil reach of the Wharfe downstream. The path concludes by rising to the road just short of Barden Bridge, and a final 'unofficial' short-lived path springs up to parallel the road, if so required.

```
┌─────────────────────────────────┐
│            ( 18 )               │
│                                  │
│        CAM  HEAD                │
└─────────────────────────────────┘
```

START Kettlewell   Grid ref. SD 968722

DISTANCE 5¾ miles

ORDNANCE SURVEY MAPS
1:50,000
Landranger 98 - Wensleydale & Upper Wharfedale
1:25,000
Outdoor Leisure 30 - Yorkshire Dales North/Central

ACCESS Start from the village centre. There is a large car park at
the entrance. Kettlewell is served by occasional buses from
Skipton via Grassington, and by seasonal services such as Dalesbus.

A splendid triangular ramble in the very heart of the upper dale:
uncomplicated and magnificently varied.

S Kettlewell is the hub of the upper dale, a junction of roads and
natural halting place. It stands on what was a major coaching route to
Richmond, and the two inns at the entrance to the village would have
serviced the weary travellers. The route in question is now a surfaced
road, but still provides a tortuous way over Park Rash and into
Coverdale. Shops, tearooms a third inn and plentiful accommodation
- including a youth hostel - add more life to a village being steadily
engulfed by holiday homes.

Kettlewell straddles its own beck which largely drains the slopes of
Great Whernside, very much Kettlewell's mountain. These slopes
bear the scars of lead mining, the one-time industry now replaced by
tourism as a partner to farming. Some delectable cottages and gardens
line the beck as it races through the village, while footpaths positively
radiate from Kettlewell to all points of the compass.

Leave the main road through the village by way of the side road heading off opposite the *Racehorses Hotel*. Cross straight over at the crossroads by the Post office/shop (signposted Leyburn) and the road soon swings left to climb out of the village. Within a minute it turns sharply right, and here leave it by continuing up the unsurfaced walled lane straight ahead. This is the Top Mere Road, which after a relatively steep start - an excuse to pause in order to admire the fine retrospective view down Wharfedale - soon eases out to become an outstanding green lane: all that is required is to tread its caressing surface.

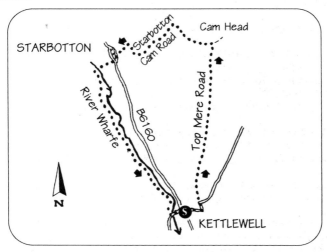

In the early stages we pass above the course of a flue from a former lead smelting mill on the floor of the adjacent side valley; while for the most part of the climb the enormous Great Whernside dominates across to the right. **Eventually all enclosing walls will be shrugged off, and the track rises across the fell to arrive at a cairn and guidepost at Cam Head.** The path running north-east from here makes for the distinctive outline of Tor Dyke, a defensive earthwork of the Iron age Brigantes tribe.

The regular appendage of 'road' names to the various green tracks of this walk is a sign of their importance in times past. Today classic walkers' highways, they originally served more functional tasks, and

71

both the contrasting styles of the Top Mere and Starbotton Cam Roads would be used to reach peat grounds and small-scale lead workings. Their well-laid courses were designed for easy descent with the spoils. The road out of Starbotton was, in addition, on a packhorse route and drove road between Coverdale and Malham.

The Top Mere Road,
looking back down Wharfedale over Kettlewell

Here at the 1706ft summit of the walk we encounter equally inviting Starbotton Road, and after a deserved sojourn, go left along this new green road for a brief level spell. After a second intervening wall, the way begins an emphatic descent to Starbotton, now as Starbotton Cam Road. Although the entire upland section of the walk is on the accommodating flanks of Buckden Pike (its massive south ridge filling 4 miles between Kettlewell and the summit), not until now are we granted a true sighting: across deeply carved Cam Gill Beck it now makes amends. During this descent the Birks Fell ridge is equally prominent as it forms the dark wall across the valley. Wharfedale here displays its finest glacial form. **As the valley floor is neared, steepening zigzags bear down on the huddled roofs of the village. A stony finish leads onto a back lane, with several options for reaching the main road.**

Starbotton sits midway between two larger and better known neighbours, Kettlewell and Buckden. Though the valley road passes through, few visitors halt here other than for refreshment at the attractive, whitewashed *Fox & Hounds*. Off the main road however are some charming corners, with 17th century cottages and a small

Quaker burial ground hidden away. Starbotton nestles comfortably under Buckden Pike, and like its neighbours stands above the river on its swift-flowing beck, which caused disastrous flooding in a deluge in 1686.

If seeking the pub bear to the right, otherwise turn along to the Kettlewell end of the village. Here a walled track heads away, running along to a footbridge across the Wharfe. Turn downstream on the opposite bank, and all is now plain sailing. This return saunter on the flat dale floor has many charms: springtime flowers; the winding ox-bows of the Wharfe; a backdrop of high fell; lovely trees; a series of typical Dales barns.... **For the most part the path - with its innumerable stiles - remains near the river and easy to follow: there are just a couple of instances where it cuts out lazy meanderings, these points being less than obvious from this direction.**

All in good time the houses of Kettlewell come into sight, though the path must adhere to the river to arrive at the road bridge at the main entrance to the village.

*The Fox & Hounds,
Starbotton*

73

19

LEA GREEN

START *Grassington*   *Grid ref. SE 002639*

DISTANCE *7 miles*

ORDNANCE SURVEY MAPS
1:50,000
Landranger 98 - Wensleydale & Upper Wharfedale
1:25,000
Outdoor Leisure 2 - Yorkshire Dales South/West

ACCESS *Start from the square in the village centre. There is a large National Park car park by the information centre on the Hebden road. Grassington is served by bus from Skipton.*

Easy walking on lush turf, with limestone features in abundance.

S Grassington is the undisputed 'capital' of the upper Wharfedale area, a thriving community with a good range of facilities. The fine, cobbled square is the focal point but it is really only the shop window: hidden away is enough interest for a day's leisurely exploration. Historically, Grassington boasted an 18th century theatre and a lead mining industry of which its nearby moor still displays much evidence. Buildings of character include the Old Hall and the former Town Hall-cum-institute. Here also is the Upper Wharfedale Folk Museum and the headquarters of the fell rescue organisation and the National Park.

From the cobbled square head up the main street past the *Devon-shire Arms*, and at the crossroads by the Town Hall go left along Chapel Street. Part way along, turn up Bank Lane on the right: this quickly swings left to level out as a walled track. Open views look to Grass Wood and the limestone pasures ahead. **At a bend take a small gate on the left, and cross a field centre to a stile. Turn left down a brow to a stile on the right, with a rough track just below (coming**

from Town Head). Turn right on this to a narrow gap-stile at the far end. The next enclosure is the site of a medieval village. **Curve to the left to a stile in the far wall, behind which a further stile admits to the great expanse of Lea Green.** These spacious pastures were the site of a vast prehistoric field system. A visit in the low light of evening will best reveal all the ancient rectangular mounds.

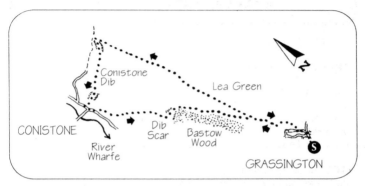

After crossing a wider track, a gentle rise leads up to join another track heading our way. A little further on a sketchy left fork is ignored, and at the brow a near-parallel wall is seen to the right. Our path refuses to fully join it until beyond a limestone pavement, when we cross to a stile just short of the corner. Note an old dewpond on the right where cattle could slake their thirsts. **Head away to a gate beyond an island outcrop and then rise to a stile, continuing up past further outcrops to a huge limekiln and a stile just over the brow. Level pastures then precede a short pull to the head of Conistone Dib.**

At the very head of the ravine leave the path for a stile on the left, and turn immediately down to a stile where a wall abuts onto a cliff. The way to Conistone is henceforward infallible, descending roughly at first before a saunter through the dry valley. Conistone Dib is a classic example of a dry limestone valley, narrowing to slender gorges at either end. **Near the foot the walls of rock close in again to form the remarkable gorge of Gurling Trough (a miniature version of Gordale Scar), through which arrival in Conistone seems very sudden.**

Cairn above Dib Scar

Conistone is an attractive, greystone little village well away from the main road, which heads updale half a mile distant, across the river at Kilnsey. Even from this distance the famous crag retains its grandeur. Every block of stone in Conistone's cottages matches the natural landscape of the village's hinterland. Though restored a century ago, the hidden church of St. Mary retains some Norman work.

On passing through the green to join the road, keep left along the back road to Grassington, and before the last house on the left turn up a rough track. Early in this stage we have a good view back over Conistone's rooftops to the dark shadow of Kilnsey Crag. **The track rises pleasantly through several pastures towards the attractive Grass and Bastow Woods directly ahead. After passing through identical corners in walls the walk's third spectacular moment reveals itself, as the ravine of Dib Scar appears at one's feet.**

Dib Scar - or simply the Dib - is another dry limestone gorge, enhanced by a backdrop of woodland, and of sufficient cragginess to have attracted climbers. Above it stands an absolute gem of a sloping pavement.

*Winter above Dib Scar:
the return path from
the outward path
on Lea Green*

The limekiln
before Conistone Dib

The path takes evasive action by swinging left to run along the rim of the dry valley. At its head a stile takes us over the wall and up the slope behind to pass through a gap in the next parallel wall. Heading directly away, a stile by a gateway is used to cross the left-hand wall, which is then followed away to the right. We are now back on the pastures of Lea Green, and on this occasion we have the delights of **Bastow Wood** just over the wall. Bastow Wood, with its lower neighbour Grass Wood, is rich in botanic interest in addition to its more obvious wooded charm.

Eventually the wall is forsaken by trending left on a green track, which descends steadily to intersect the outward route just above the stile onto Lea Green. Here leave the track to drop down to the stile to retrace steps into Grassington.

In Conistone Dib

20

HAZLEWOOD MOOR

START Bolton Abbey   Grid ref. SE 077552

DISTANCE 6 miles

ORDNANCE SURVEY MAPS
1:50,000
Landranger 104 - Leeds, Bradford & Harrogate
1:25,000
Outdoor Leisure 2 - Yorkshire Dales South/West

ACCESS Start from the Cavendish Pavilion, signposted off the
B6160 just north of Bolton Abbey, turning off by the large
memorial fountain. It has a large car park. The B6265 is served by
Skipton-Bolton Abbey-Grassington buses and seasonal Dalesbus.

A high level circuit of Pickles Gill on moorland tracks. Navigational
errors on this walk can only be major ones: while heather is all around,
it need never be actually underfoot!

• IMPORTANT The whole of this moorland known as Barden Fell is
part of the Duke of Devonshire's estate, and is the subject of an access
agreement. Above the minor road through Storiths we are on access
land (or permissive paths thereto) which may be closed on certain
days during the grouse shooting season (not Sundays) and at times of
high fire risk. Notices are posted at the access point, but for advance
information, contact Grassington National Park Centre or the estate
office. Dogs are not allowed on the access area.

🅢 Hazlewood Moor is only a part of this vast upland stretching east
to Thruscross, but - Simon's Seat aside - it does not attract the numbers
of walkers that tramp over Barden Moor across the Wharfe. It is
curious to note that even on the moor, more time is spent on paths
serving the access area than in the area itself.

Bolton Abbey is, strictly, the name of the tiny village whose show-piece is more correctly the priory. This imposing ruin is a magnet for nearby West Yorkshire visitors, with the river itself being a major attraction hereabouts. The priory was founded by Augustinian canons who moved here in 1154 from Embsay. At the Dissolution the nave was spared, and to this day remains the parish church. Of further interest is Bolton Hall, a 17th century shooting lodge; and a large and magnificent tithe barn.

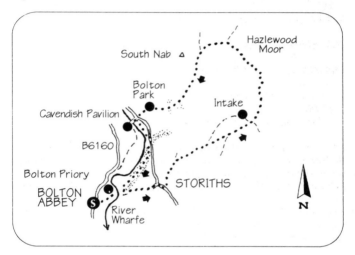

Leave the road through Bolton Abbey by the famous 'Hole in the Wall' by the Post office, and descend with the crowds to the ever lovely environs of the priory ruins. A look round might be better enjoyed at the end of the walk, so for now cross the wooden footbridge and turn upstream. Almost at once the main path bears right to gently scale the hillside. At the first opportunity take the branch doubling back up to the right to the top of the wood. Here a narrow, deeply inurned snicket whisks us away from the Bolton Abbey scene, climbing to Bank Farm and then up its road to meet the minor road through Storiths.

Storiths is an unassuming little settlement, so near and yet so far from Bolton Abbey's crowds. Just along to the left, at Back 'o th' Hill Farm a coffee shop marries refreshments with a model railway gallery.

Across the road is the pocket moor of Storiths Crag, and on turning a short distance up to the right, a stony drive heads off by the wall-side. This is the start of an extended route onto the Barden Fell access area, though within only a couple of minutes we will be on open moor. Approaching Town End Farm, bear right over a cattle-grid onto the moor, and a little further bear right at a fork for the track to begin a steady pull towards the heights.

As height is gained the intake wall returns, and at another fork (Intake farm drive) our route takes the initially less appealing way to the right. This green track soon perks up to head straight on as a similar track comes in from the right. Down to the left are a handful of fields encircling Intake Farm, and when a track climbs from it to briefly join us, take no notice as it quickly resumes its climb to the right (here we enter the access area). Our route now begins a cautious drop towards Pickles Gill Beck, reaching the stream at a sheepfold in a setting that begs a refreshment halt.

The 'Hole in the Wall', Bolton Abbey

The path makes a short, steep climb from the fold before easing out to undulate along to a junction. At 1115ft, this is the highest point of the walk. **Go down to the left to arrive at Hammerthorn Gate.** On the knoll to the right an Ordnance Survey column set well back from South Nab may tempt a detour. **Continue down the stony track: at the next gate we leave the access area. The track descends through green pastures to the hugely attractive farmhouse of Bolton Park. Passing to the right of the buildings its drive leads down to the Storiths-Barden road.**

Cross straight over to the wooden bridge over the Wharfe. Arrival at the Cavendish Pavilion is a severe culture shock after the open moor! **If not succumbing to the various temptations over the bridge, then take the riverbank path downstream. At the far end of the pasture we are deflected onto the road to negotiate Pickles Beck, with a hidden footbridge upstream of the ford. On the other side two paths plunge into the riverside woods: both lead unfailingly back to the priory footbridge, though the higher one offers a more rewarding trek.**

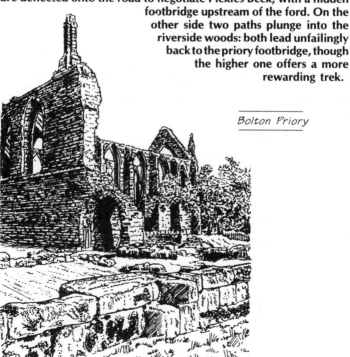

Bolton Priory

81

21

BURNSALL

START Linton Falls   Grid ref. SE 001631

DISTANCE 6¼ miles

ORDNANCE SURVEY MAPS
1:50,000
Landranger 98 - Wensleydale & Upper Wharfedale
1:25,000
Outdoor Leisure 2 - Yorkshire Dales South/West

ACCESS Start from the National Park car park on the cul-de-sac road to Linton church. The walk can also be easily started from Grassington or Burnsall, both served by bus from Skipton.

An undemanding walk clinging tightly to the river after an outward leg offering fine Wharfedale views.

S **From the car park head along the road towards the church, but if saving its charm for the end of the walk, turn up a short enclosed way before a house on the right. At the end (ignoring another way branching off it) a pasture is entered, and crossed to a stile on the left of the barn ahead. From it rise diagonally up above the steeper drop to arrive at a stile in the distant facing wall. Two slender fields then precede emergence onto the Burnsall road.**

Turn right a few yards to a gate opposite and rise half left to a gate in a fence. Slightly left again takes us to an elusive hand-gate, behind which a narrow green snicket wends its way up to join the similarly narrow Thorpe Lane. In an uncharacteristic lapse the Ordnance Survey have omitted to portray the snicket as the enclosed way it has clearly been for a long, long time. **Go left into Thorpe.** The farming hamlet of Thorpe has an elusiveness that is legend, for it quite likely kept its people and their livestock hidden from marauding Scots. Romantically but appropriately titled Thorpe in the Hollow, it shelters between reef knolls and below the overpowering Thorpe Fell, part of Barden Moor. A wooded enclosure forms the village 'centre'.

From the centre bear left past the last of the buildings. Just a little further, leave the road by a rough lane on the right: at its early demise drop down through a slender field to an intervening fence and down again to a stile by a trickling stream. The way rises away in a virtual straight line, across a trio of fields to reach the unsurfaced Badger Lane.

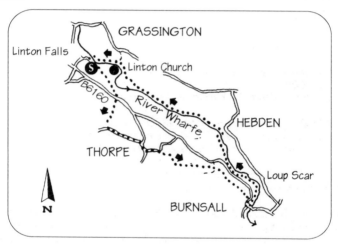

A stile opposite resumes the fields' crossing, and after dropping down the first field a direct course for Burnsall is set. The church tower makes a useful guide, while behind it, Simon's Seat dominates the skyline. **More guidance is provided by a tightly bunched series of stiles, designed to test one's agility in addition to deferring arrival in Burnsall. The village is entered by way of a back yard, then turning right along the street into the centre.**

Burnsall's setting is one of near perfection, with bridge, green - and maypole - church, inn and cottages fusing into an unforgettable Wharfedale scene. The church is just outside the centre, but worth a short walk up the road past the post office. It dates largely from the

15th century, and has an inscribed Norman font - note also the functional lych-gate. Alongside is another lovely building, the village school, founded in 1602 as one of the earliest grammar schools.

Join the Wharfe by turning down between the *Red Lion* and the bridge, and follow a path upstream. It soon sees the back of the village, passing below the church and along to a knoll above the gorge of Loup Scar. Here the Wharfe rushes through an impressive limestone fault, a hugely popular short stroll. **In these spectacular environs the path drops back down to the river to run through charming wooded surroundings to the suspension bridge below Hebden.** Just before reaching it, note the old stone stairway known as the 'Postman's Steps'. The suspension bridge celebrated its centenary in 1985, having been constructed to replace stepping stones.

Loup Scar, Burnsall

On the opposite bank this uncomplicated leg of the walk resumes, through a deeply inurned reach of the Wharfe. On emerging, a loop in the river is cut out by striking across a large pasture to the right of the tree masked sewage works. At its access road a direct option crosses the stepping stones ahead to reach the church. **If baulked, turn right along the track away from the river and up past a fish farm. As it climbs through a bend, take a stile on the left to regain the Wharfe's bank opposite Linton church. A couple of fields further and the footbridge at Linton Falls is reached.**

84

At Linton Falls the Wharfe erupts into a rare moment of anger as it tumbles over limestone boulders and ledges, a foaming sight in spate. The bridge makes a perfect vantage point. This 1989 replacement for the part iron bridge that itself replaced the original structure is unlikely to see the affectionately held name 'Tin Bridge' forgotten. Another change was the demolition, to make way for housing in the mid 1980s, of a large mill that stood adjacent to the bridge. In contrast to the turbulent falls, immediately upstream the river flows wide and calm between two weirs. **To conclude, a ginnel leads back onto the road with the car park just along to the left.**

The old Tin Bridge, Linton Falls

To visit the church, keep on past the car park to the road's demise. Enclosed in a serene loop of the river is the squat church of St. Michael and all Angels, so positioned as to be central to the several villages it was built to serve. Dating from Norman times, it retains much 15th century work and its interior lives up to its idyllic setting.

22

SKYREHOLME

START *Stump Cross*   *Grid ref. SE 086635*

DISTANCE *7½ miles*

ORDNANCE SURVEY MAPS
1:50,000
Landranger 99 - Northallerton & Ripon
1:25,000
Outdoor Leisure 2 - Yorkshire Dales South/West

ACCESS *Start from a large lay-by below the steep bend in the road just beneath Stump Cross Caverns (which also has a large car park). Alternative start: Grimwith Reservoir car park.*

A fascinatingly varied trek along a series of old tracks. Trollers Gill is one of many natural features. Skyreholme and Dry Gill provide a rare choice of isolated country tearooms.

S Stump Cross Caverns, one of only three showcaves in the Dales, were discovered in 1860 by unsuspecting miners seeking lead. Revealed was an amazing labyrinth of tunnels and chambers, with a display of stalactites and stalagmites that cannot fail to impress. The bleak exterior and setting give no clues to the wonders underground. It is open March to November and winter weekends.

At the foot of the steep pull to the caverns, a path leaves the road at a small pocket of open ground. After a stile it quickly shakes off its accompanying wall and rises to the foot of prominent Nursery Knot. The path passes behind the outcrop, but few will resist a closer look. Nursery Knot is a limestone knoll with sweeping views across the reservoir to Great Whernside, and at 1276ft is, already, the highest point of the walk. **At the wall corner behind, two adjacent stiles can be taken in tandem without touching the ground before a line of stakes point the way to Grimwith Reservoir. These stakes maintain**

the route down through several rough enclosures before crossing two fields to a stile onto the reservoir road. Grimwith Reservoir is, after enlargement in the 1980s, a vast sheet of water held by a surprisingly unobtrusive grassy dam. Public access has been increased by the provision of parking and quiet water sports facilities, while the now submerged path has been replaced so that a circuit of the reservoir can still be made (see WALK 30).

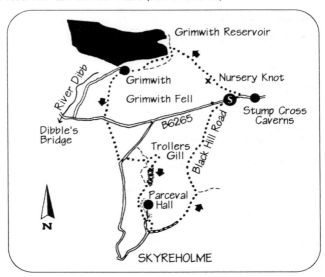

Go left along the hard track round the water's edge. On the right is the cruck framed, heather thatched High Laithe Barn. **Just beyond, a path breaks off to run nearer the shore before climbing back to the track. A little further along, the road runs into the car park: turn up the drive between toilets and houses, and from the gate above a track runs along to the Pateley Bridge road.** This moorland track is the original access road to the farms of Grimwith House and Gate Up, either abandoned or drowned by the arrival of the deep waters. It offers a sweeping panorama over Wharfedale to Barden Moor.

Cross straight over onto a green lane, soon losing an enclosing wall to run an idyllic course to join New Road on a bend. Go left a few yards to a stile from where an unclear path bears half-left: soon it drops to a hollow on the left to meet a wide track. En route it passes a dark

87

slit that is the entrance to Hell Hole. Turn briefly right on this old mine road: the public footpath runs through this deep side valley with its old lead mining site, as Trollers Gill, hidden behind the high wedge of Middle Hill, is not on a definitive right of way. However, as long as it is remains accessible under the Countryside Stewardship scheme, then bear left off the track on a thin path over the brow, slanting north-east to drop down to tiny Skyreholme Beck, upstream of the ravine. Across the stile and beck turn downstream, and after another stile the path enters the ravine proper, emerging by some springs at the southern entrance.

Trollers Gill is a magnificent limestone gorge, known as the 'Gordale of Wharfedale'. Though not particularly tall, the cliffs remain virtually unbroken for some distance (illustrated on page 39). The narrow passage between is usually dry and safe, but it is renowned as home of the legendary *Barguest*, a spectral hound with eyes like saucers! **The path heads away to rejoin the public path. Re-united, the way runs on past the prominent site of a dam that burst in 1899, and the charming green path traces Skyreholme Beck down to emerge onto the drive to Parceval Hall.** The grandest house in Upper Wharfedale was built over 300 years ago: its beautiful stonework looks out across Skyreholme to Simon's Seat, which totally dominates this corner of the valley. Now used as a diocesan retreat centre, the gardens and woodland are open to view from Easter to October (small charge).

Cross the bridge and from a stile in the yard corner head across the field with a wall. At the second gateway enter a field on the right to drop diagonally to a gate by the road to Skyreholme. Turn left for a long, steady pull up Skyreholme Bank before the road finally loses its surface. Keep left at a fork a little further on, and continue over the brow on the welcoming green surface of Black Hill Road. In time it drops down towards Dry Gill (passing above a cave) to join the Pateley Bridge road just down from the starting point.

Nursery Knot, looking over Black Hill Road to Simon's Seat

23

LANGSTROTHDALE

START *Buckden*   *Grid ref. SD 942772*

DISTANCE *6 miles*

ORDNANCE SURVEY MAPS
1:50,000
Landranger 98 - Wensleydale & Upper Wharfedale
1:25,000
Outdoor Leisure 30 - Yorkshire Dales North/Central

ACCESS *Start from the village centre. There is a large National Park car park. Served by infrequent buses from Skipton via Grassington, and by seasonal services such as Dalesbus.*

Very easy walking in the unspoilt and ravishingly beautiful environs of the infant Wharfe. The walk can be shortened to 3½ miles by a Hubberholme start, but there is only limited riverside parking.

S   Buckden is the first sizeable settlement encountered by the Wharfe, at the meeting place of two high roads from Wensleydale. The B6160 comes via Cray to take over from the narrow, winding strip of tarmac that reaches nearly 2000ft on its way over Fleet Moss from Hawes, before running through Langstrothdale to Buckden. In medieval times Buckden was the centre of a vast hunting forest, and its hostelry recalls its former importance in its name. The village stands high above the river on the slopes of Buckden Pike, and swift-flowing Buckden Beck carves a deep defile down from the summit.

Leave by the Hawes road descending from the green, and immediately over the bridge take the riverside path on the right. This traces the Wharfe upstream until ushered back onto the road. A half-mile stretch leads into Hubberholme.

Barely even a hamlet, Hubberholme boasts two famous buildings and a shapely bridge which connects them. The church of St. Michael is a gem, its tower showing Norman traces. Its best feature is a 500-year old oak rood loft, one of only two remaining in Yorkshire, while some pews bear the famous trademark of 'Mousy' Thompson. Carving therefore - both ancient and modern - dominates the interior of this highest church in the dale. Outside, meanwhile, the sparkling Wharfe runs almost past its very door. Across the river is the whitewashed and homely *George Inn* in an idyllic setting. Formerly housing the vicar, its flagged floors continue to be the scene of the New Year 'land-letting' when proceeds of a 'poor pasture' go to needy parishioners.

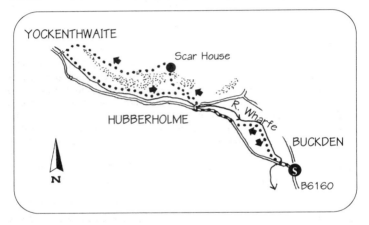

Cross the bridge and take a gate adjacent to the church, from where a broad drive climbs to Scar House. Restored in the 19th century, isolated Scar House was the scene of early Quaker gatherings. **Passing between the buildings, turn left at the top to a stile by a gate, from where a sketchy path sets an obvious course through the minor outcrops of a limestone shelf.**

Through this section we enjoy level walking with outstanding views over the youthful Wharfe in Langstrothdale to the Birks Fell-Horse Head ridge which forms a bulky wall opposite. Note the 'toytown' appearance of the farm settlement at Raisgill tucked hard under the fell.

The bridge, Yockenthwaite

Through a small wood the path crosses over Strans Gill. Under this limestone ravine lurks a complex caving system. **The path then slants half-left before maintaining a level traverse through numerous walls in various conditions. Further on, it is diverted to slant down to a wall before running on through more trees to emerge on a scarred track above Yockenthwaite. The track drops down to the farming hamlet in its magnificent setting.** 'Eogan's clearing' was named by the Norsemen who settled here. Much later, all this area was once part of the hunting forest of Langstrothdale Chase. Up to more recent times the small community supported both an inn and a school.

Without crossing the shapely bridge our return route doubles back down to a gate above the river. Quickly on the bank of the Wharfe no further instructions need be given, the path shadowing the river back to Hubberholme, and emerging onto the outward track behind the church. Retrace steps back to Buckden to finish.

The George Inn,
Hubberholme

24

LANGCLIFFE EDGE

START Kettlewell   Grid ref. SD 968722

DISTANCE 5¾ miles

ORDNANCE SURVEY MAPS
1:50,000
Landranger 98 - Wensleydale & Upper Wharfedale
1:25,000
Outdoor Leisure 2 - Yorkshire Dales South/West
          30 - Yorkshire Dales North/Central

ACCESS Start from the village centre. There is a large car park at the entrance. Kettlewell is served by occasional buses from Skipton via Grassington and by seasonal Dalesbus.

Former lead mines offer an interesting addition to the meeting of limestone and gritstone in Kettlewell's hinterland.

S Kettlewell is the hub of the upper dale, a junction of roads and natural halting place. It stands on what was a major coaching route to Richmond, and the two inns at the entrance to the village would have serviced the weary travellers. The route in question is now a surfaced road, but still provides a tortuous way over Park Rash and into Coverdale. Shops, tearooms a third inn and plentiful accommodation - including a youth hostel - add more life to a village being steadily engulfed by holiday homes.

Kettlewell straddles its own beck which largely drains the slopes of Great Whernside, very much Kettlewell's mountain. These slopes bear the scars of lead mining, the one-time industry now replaced by tourism as a partner to farming. Some delectable cottages and gardens line the beck as it races through the village. Footpaths positively radiate from Kettlewell to all points of the compass.

From the car park head into the village, and turn on the road to the right before the bridge and hotels. Fork left at the maypole to pass between the *King's Head* and the church and straight on along a narrow lane parallel with the beck. Just before a shapely bridge carries the road back over the beck, turn steeply up to the right on a stony bridleway.

The roughness underfoot soon gives way to an ever improving grassy track as the gradient eases. Intervening fence and wall precede a winding course up a large pasture to reach a higher parallel wall, From where a short lived way between crumbling walls climbs further. As one wall expires the track effects a zigzag up to the left, then crosses two virtually level pastures to the moor gate and attendant stile.

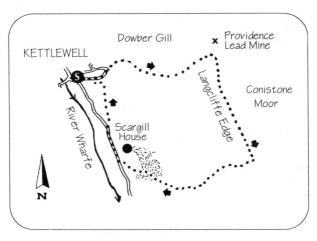

Just down to the left are the remains of the Providence lead mine. It was one of the largest in the district, and its immediate environs are littered with abandoned shafts and bell-pits. The centre of operations is found down towards Dowber Gill Beck, and our track to the moor gate would once have been busy with loads of ore won from the mine. The old workings are - as indeed is the entire walk - on the broad flanks of Great Whernside, which asserts its full stature across Dowber Gill Beck during the climb.

Our route turns uphill with the wall for a short pull to a prominent stand of cairns. These stone sentinels are craftsman built from the plentiful supply of gritstone. They mark a fine viewpoint for the mountains of the southern Dales, with Penyghent prominent. Almost at the upper limit of the walk we witness the transition from limestone to gritstone, giving a nice change of scene for the stroll along the 1700ft contour.

Buckden Pike from the Providence cairns

From here on the route, while only a sketchy path, remains infallible as the only requirement is to accompany the wall along the well defined Langcliffe Edge, with Conistone Moor above us. A good mile of walking brings arrival at a ladder-stile by a gate, signalling the commencement of the return leg.

The chapel, Scargill House

On the other side a wide panorama over Wharfedale greets the eye. **A grand track drops down, initially steeply, towards limestone pastures. Passing through a collapsed wall it winds down through a very long pasture, becoming indistinct but aiming for the bottom right corner. From the gate there an improving track slants down to a similar point at the edge of a plantation. Known as Highgate Leys Lane it descends the hillside, passing near Scargill House before turning left to emerge onto the Kettlewell-Conistone road.** The familiar landmark of the chapel at Scargill House blends surprisingly well into its setting. The house is a retreat and conference centre.

Turn right past the drive to Scargill House, then after a couple of kinks in the narrow lane take a gate by a footpath sign on the right. Head away to a gateway then turn through it to a gate in the next wall to commence a fascinating course through about a dozen fields within half a mile. Though not visible on the ground, the way follows a near straight wall, twice switching sides before emerging at the head of a narrow green lane on the edge of the village. Turn down it to a T-junction, and then right onto a back lane on which the walk began.

Upper Wharfedale from above Highgate Leys Lane, with Old Cote Moor (left), Yockenthwaite Moor and the slopes of Buckden Pike

95

25

BUCKDEN PIKE

START *Buckden*   *Grid ref. SD 942772*

DISTANCE *8½ miles*

ORDNANCE SURVEY MAPS
1:50,000
Landranger 98 - Wensleydale & Upper Wharfedale
1:25,000
Outdoor Leisure 30 - Yorkshire Dales North/Central

ACCESS *Start from the village centre. There is a large National Park car park. Buckden is served by occasional bus from Skipton via Grassington and by seasonal Dalesbus.*

A well-graded and popular climb to Wharfedale's second highest summit, with the bonus of a beautiful riverside return.

S   Buckden is the first sizeable settlement encountered by the Wharfe, and stands at the meeting place of two high roads from Wensleydale to the north. The good quality B6160 comes via Cray to take over as the valley road from the narrow, winding strip of tarmac that reaches nearly 2000ft on its way over Fleet Moss from Hawes, before running through Langstrothdale to Buckden. In medieval times Buckden was the centre of a vast hunting forest, and its hostelry recalls its former importance in its name. The village stands high above the river on the slope of Buckden Pike, and swift-flowing Buckden Beck carves a deep defile down from the summit.

Leave the car park not by its usual exit, but by a gate at its northern end, from where a stony track makes its way gently up Buckden Rake. This is one of the few confirmed sections of the Roman road that connected the forts at Ilkley and Bainbridge. It remains an excellent

96

route to this day, and provides a perfect picture of the dale head scene, looking beyond Hubberholme's church tower into Langstrothdale. As we leave it to climb, note the hamlet of Cray below. **When the surround of trees disappears, the track turns right through a gate and onto the level.**

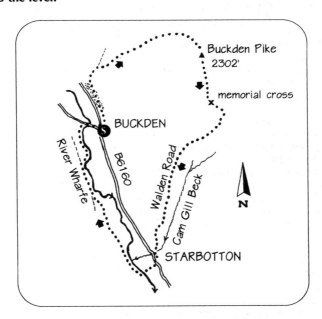

From the next gate however, our chosen path forks right to resume the upward push. This generally clear path rises diagonally through five pastures, and beyond the last of them it heads more directly up the open fell. A little sketchily and in part marshily it crosses to a wall on the left, to then accompany it up to the cairn and Ordnance Survey column on the summit of Buckden Pike.

At 2302ft, Buckden Pike's virtues as a viewpoint are in its distant prospects, which are truly extensive. Most of the major Dales' summits are visible in the western sector, while to the east, moors give way to the flat plains. On a clear day the Cleveland Hills can be seen rising beyond the void.

To leave the top use the stile to cross the boundary wall and turn right to follow it along the broad ridge of the pike. This regularly used path linking the summit and the Walden Road is not currently recorded as a definitive right of way. **Little height is lost as a memorial cross is passed.** This noble structure was erected by a Polish airman, lone survivor of a second world war plane crash on the fell. **At the foot of the slope behind it the track known as the Walden Road is met at a sharp angle in the wall.** This former packhorse route continues over the fell to drop down to the head of the lonely Walden Valley and ultimately Wensleydale. Just along it to the left is an inscribed boundary stone. **Use the bridle-gate to re-cross the wall and commence the descent to Starbotton.**

This is at such a gentle gradient that one's time can be fully employed in enjoying the splendid views down Wharfedale. **The way is fairly clear throughout: after sloping down across two large, rough pastures linked by a little mining debris, a cracking pace can be adopted as the track descends parallel with Cam Gill Beck to our left. Starbotton is entered via a bridge onto a lane, which leads to the right and onto the main road by the *Fox and Hounds*.**

Situated midway between better known Kettlewell and Buckden, tiny Starbotton witnesses all that passes through the dale, even though only a small number pause here. The usual reason for halting is to visit the attractive, whitewashed pub. Off the main road are some lovely corners with 17th century cottages, including a 1665 datestone opposite the pub. Like its neighbours Starbotton stands away from the river on its own swift-flowing beck. Cam Gill Beck cuts a deep groove in the flank of the pike, and in 1686 was swollen by a deluge which caused disastrous flooding in the village.

The Wharfe between Starbotton and Buckden

The summit of Buckden Pike, looking over the Birks Fell ridge to Penyghent and Ingleborough

Turn left through the village, and after the last building leave the road by an enclosed track on the right, which leads to a footbridge over the Wharfe. Cross it and turn right to follow the river upstream to commence the return to Buckden. When the Wharfe temporarily parts company the path continues straight ahead alongside a wall on the left: several stiles and gates interrupt the journey. As the river returns a wide track is joined, but as the Wharfe bends away again this time go with it to remain on its bank until Buckden Bridge is encountered. Here leave the river and cross the bridge to re-enter the village.

The Memorial Cross, Buckden Pike

26

HORSE HEAD PASS

START *Halton Gill*   *Grid ref. SD 880764*

DISTANCE *8 miles*

ORDNANCE SURVEY MAPS
1:50,000
Landranger 98 - Wensleydale & Upper Wharfedale
1:25,000
Outdoor Leisure 30 - Yorkshire Dales North/Central

ACCESS *Start in the centre of the hamlet. There is reasonable parking, notably the lay-by opposite the green.*

A stiff inter valley walk in the heart of the Dales. The filling is a couple of peerless miles in the company of the infant Wharfe, in Langstrothdale. Save it for a clear day.

◐   Halton Gill is the first settlement of any size in Littondale. Its cluster of greystone buildings include a centuries-old chapel and even a grammar school, but both are now private dwellings. **Leave the green by the up-dale (Foxup) road, and beyond a bend after the last buildings take a gate on the right, rather ambitiously signposted to Hawes.**

At the outset (and also the conclusion) of the walk, the bird's-eye views of Halton Gill are first-rate. During the climb, the famous Three Peaks appear in turn, Ingleborough at the first turning; Penyghent at the crossing of Halton Gill Beck; and Whernside between there and Horse Head Gate. **A broad track slopes up the field, and this same track remains our route, with little effort and no complications, to the summit of the Horse Head Pass on the broad top of this mighty ridge.**

100

Just along to the left is the Ordnance Survey column (S5496) at 1984ft, one of several 'tops' along the crest of this mighty ridge between Littondale and Upper Wharfedale. The pass itself climbs little short of the ridge's highest point, which narrowly fails to make the 2000ft mark on Birks Fell further east. The well-made green road over the pass was a regular route of Halton Gill's curate, who rode over on horseback each Sunday to take the service at Hubberholme.

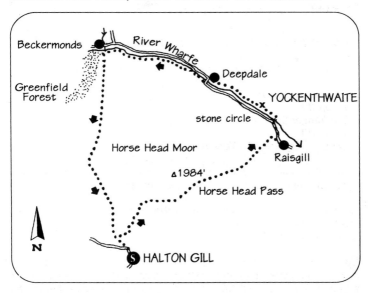

Descent to the promised land of Langstrothdale is equally straight-forward, the track heading directly away from the wall and soon dropping more directly and less skilfully towards Hagg Beck. These delightful environs herald the welcome appearance of limestone: its attendant bracken and gnarled trees add colour and character to the backdrop of Yockenthwaite Moor and Buckden Pike. The deeply carved gill also holds sufficient interest for cavers. **After this stretch the descent concludes at the unfenced road near Raisgill Farm.**

Turn down to the left the short distance to Yockenthwaite. A graceful bridge leads to this farming hamlet in a magnificent setting. 'Eogan's clearing' was named by the Norsemen who settled here. Much later, all this area was once part of the hunting forest of Langstrothdale Chase. Up to more recent times the small community supported both an inn and a school. **Cross the bridge and on rising to the first building turn sharp left to a gate. Here commences a magnificent ramble in the effervescent company of the infant Wharfe.**

After a couple of pastures the track fades as it passes Yockenthwaite stone circle. This compact grouping of 30 stones is of modest proportion, but in a noble riverside setting easily missed by travellers on the road. **From a stile beyond it a faint path materialises to rise slightly away from the river through a wall gap to another stile. Cross the field-top to a footbridge at the other side, then on through a gap and a gate to join the access road to Deepdale. Turn down to the road and cross the uninspiring bridge to keep the road at bay.**

Yockenthwaite Stone Circle

A track sets forth up the west bank as far as lonely New House, from where a footpath keeps faith with the river as far as a wooden footbridge opposite the farm buildings of Beckermonds. Beckermonds presides over the meeting of Oughtershaw and Greenfield Becks - the creation of the Wharfe, no less. This confluence below Beckermonds Bridge is well seen from our approach to the footbridge, a charming spot. Each beck has already covered some mileage to provide a fair volume of water for the Wharfe's birth. The Greenfield Forest is home to a herd of roe deer.

However, our route must make its way back over the ridge, the climb beginning from a gate on the left just short of reaching the bridge and a forestry plantation. A sketchy track starts a direct climb adjacent to a tiny beck, rising past a barn to trace the near side of the beck.

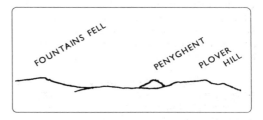

Looking south
from Horse
Head Gate

FOUNTAINS FELL

PENYGHENT

PLOVER HILL

Necessary breaks in this return climb provide wide vistas over the incomparably bleak head of Wharfedale. **When the beck acquires a distinct grassy ravine, keep above it to then follow a string of occasional, discreet cairns on a march up the fellside. At a series of shakeholes the path becomes fainter still, but once regained (note the cairn on one of the topmost boulders) is reasonably easy to follow up the higher slopes. An odd peat grough is encountered before the going eases and a well-constructed stone man on a platform is reached. The ridge wall at 1873ft is now visible beyond, and a stile therein quickly gained.**

On the other side the path briefly remains level, then turns sharply down to the left to pass through a long-collapsed wall and meet a level trod. Turn left along it, maintaining the contour to run past a guidepost to a ladder-stile. Remaining level a little further, and crossing over a climbing path, our path improves into a fine green way as it drops down through a modest rock gateway to a hollow above an area of limestone outcrops. From a stile in the wall ahead a sketchier continuation slants down to the far corner of the enclosure, beyond which outward steps are retraced back down into Halton Gill.

Stone man, Horse Head Ridge

103

27

MASTILES LANE

START Kilnsey   Grid ref. SD 974677

DISTANCE 7¾ miles

ORDNANCE SURVEY MAPS
1:50,000
Landranger 98 - Wensleydale & Upper Wharfedale
1:25,000
Outdoor Leisure 2 - Yorkshire Dales South/West

ACCESS Start from the Tennant Arms. Parking is limited to the vicinity of the inn: at the front is patrons only. The more capacious Kilnsey Park is also 'patrons only'. There is also room at Conistone Bridge, at the end of the route. Kilnsey is served by occasional buses from Skipton via Grassington, and by seasonal Dalesbus.

A famous green road through extensive limestone uplands.

S   Kilnsey offers attractions far outweighing its modest hamlet status. It is renowned first and foremost, of course, for the stupendous rock architecture of Kilnsey Crag, whose only fault is its almost unnatural roadside location. It is a favourite climbing ground, and motorists frequently screech to a halt to weigh up the progress of rock gymnasts. After rain a clutch of springs gush exhuberantly from the base of the cliffs, whose famous overhang can brood for only one day in 365 over Kilnsey's other great draw, its show. At the back end of summer the riverside pasture across the road is alive with the colour of the dale's premier event. As with most agricultural shows, the attractions are boosted by such long-standing Kilnsey specialities as trotting and fell running. No prizes are offered for guessing the destination of the latter, the senior race being a major event in itself: in 1978 we stood at the top to see the legendary Fred Reeves of Coniston touch the highest flag before turning for victory.

Other aspects of Kilnsey range from a centuries-old hall to a modern trout farm. The latter, along with the *Anglers' Arms* which stood almost cheek by jowl with the surviving hostelry until some decades ago, is a firm pointer to another of Kilnsey's traditions. The Old Hall was built in Tudor times on the site of a grange of Fountains Abbey: now a ruin, it may well be restored before too long. Kilnsey Park has established itself in recent years as a visitor attraction. Its features include a nature trail, trout fishing, aquarium, shop and restaurant.

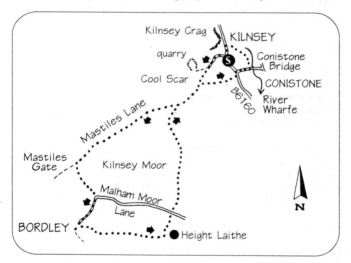

Leave the main road by a side road just to the south of the *Tennant Arms*, climbing out of the hamlet by the restored Old Hall. This is an unspectacular start to the 'big name' in green roads of the Dales, Mastiles Lane. Riding the rolling limestone uplands, it gave access to the valuable sheep grazing grounds of Malham for the Fountains' monks, indeed continuing ultimately to their lands in Borrowdale, in Cumberland. Packmen and drovers would have taken advantage of it, though the confining walls that seem integral to its atmosphere would not have been known to its monastic patrons. **The road remains surfaced to approach Coolscar Quarry, which rates high in the eyesore league. Fortunately it is escaped by a more inviting track branching left before the quarry entrance. The famous lane now remains our chosen course for a considerable time.**

Passing below the low line of Cool Scar, the old road runs unenclosed a short distance before the walls close in at a depression: on the descent thereto the road can be surveyed ahead, climbing impressively to the skyline. Here the walk reaches its highest point at 1388ft. On eventually gaining this brow, the way drops down to Mastiles Gate, and as the road runs free again we must leave it by turning left on a grassy wall-side track.

At the other end a crossroads with the terminus of a surfaced road is reached: cross straight over and head up the access road to Bordley. On the brow it becomes surfaced again to drop down to the hamlet. Bordley is a lonely outpost where sheep farming continues from its days as a monastic township. Its immediate environs provide our only incursion into the gathering grounds of neighbouring Airedale.

Winter on Mastiles Lane

Just before the gate to enter its confines however, turn off left above a wall, bearing left at the end to locate a stile by a wall corner. From it climb - wall-side again - the short, steep pull opposite, and at the brow keep straight on along a sketchy but fairly obvious course. The route maintains a straight line through the pasture beneath limestone scars high to the left, and soon encounters a battery of stiles set in parallel walls. From the last one aim straight ahead to a barn in the corner, where a stile deposits onto a short-lived enclosed track above Height Laithe. In this last enclosure note the tiny beck disappearing at Higher Height Holes on the right, and the splendidly preserved limekiln over to the left. On gaining the green way above Height Laithe, note also the twin black entrances to Calf Hole (or Height Cave) eastwards. It has revealed important evidences of occupation by Bronze and Iron age man.

Head left along the green track, which soon breaks free to cross a pasture to the Threshfield-Bordley road (Malham Moor Lane). Directly opposite another track heads off, rising gently to a minor brow before dropping to a gate in an intervening wall. Descent from Kilnsey Moor is by way of a grand track that takes a natural course through a dry shallow valley in this vast sheep pasture. This long descent of the moor allows sweeping panoramas over Wharfedale. Ahead are the dale's twin giants of Buckden Pike and Great Whernside, while lower down we enjoy a complete picture of the limestone country above Conistone.

Eventually the track winds down to the left, with a brief enclosed spell preceding rejoining Mastiles Lane. A direct return to Kilnsey simply involves retracing the first mile of the walk, but a more interesting conclusion can be enjoyed by locating a slender stile at a kink in the adjacent wall below Cool Scar. From it descend to a barn, from where an access track heads away to run steadily down to the main road.

Go left a few yards along the road before escaping along the quieter Conistone road. Just before bridging the Wharfe a stile admits to the large pasture on the left, and initially a clear track heads away. When it fades by a wall corner bear away from the river, skirting another corner en route to the prominent barn of Scar Lathe beneath the hugely imposing wall of Kilnsey Crag itself. Here the road is rejoined, and after appraising the cliff turn left for the short walk back into Kilnsey.

Kilnsey Crag

28

SIMON'S SEAT
from Appletreewick

START *Appletreewick*   *Grid ref. SE 053601*

DISTANCE *6½ miles*

ORDNANCE SURVEY MAPS
1:50,000
Landranger 98 - Wensleydale & Upper Wharfedale
*   99 - Northallerton & Ripon*
*   104 - Leeds, Bradford & Harrogate*
1:25,000
Outdoor Leisure 2 - Yorkshire Dales South/West

ACCESS *Start from the village centre. During the season a large riverside field near the village centre provides car parking. Other than this, parking is somewhat limited. Served by Skipton-Bolton Abbey-Grassington buses and seasonal Dalesbus.*

This is Simon's Seat 'the hard way'. Unremitting flanks divide open moorland and pastoral valley floor. The effort will be well repaid.

• *IMPORTANT* Simon's Seat is part of the expanse of moorland known as Barden Fell, and is part of the Duke of Devonshire's estate. From Howgill to Dale Head we are on access land (or permissive paths thereto) which may be closed on certain days during the grouse shooting season (not Sundays) and at times of high fire risk. Notices are posted at the access points, but for advance information, contact either Grassington National Park Centre or the estate office. Dogs are not allowed on the access area.

S Appletreewick has several claims to fame, even though many visitors may best remember its delightful name. Here are three halls and two inns in amongst a wonderful assortment of cottages. All stand on or about the narrow road wandering through the village, from High Hall at the top - note the tiny St. John's church nearby - to Low Hall at the very bottom. Probably the oldest however is Mock Beggar Hall, a fine little edifice that once went by the title of Monk's Hall.

Of the two pubs, the *Craven Arms* takes its name from the family of William Craven, a Dick Whittington character who found fortune in London, becoming Lord Mayor in 1611. Not forgetting his beginnings he became a worthy local benefactor, having Burnsall's grammar school and a number of bridges in the district built. The *New Inn*, meanwhile, achieved national fame in the 1970s thanks to the enterprising 'no-smoking' policy of the then landlord. Since then it has been equally enterprising in its extensive range of beers from abroad.

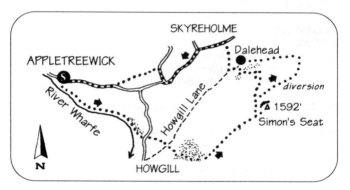

Leave the village by the Burnsall road, past the pubs and Low Hall to find a walled path leading down to the Wharfe. Turn left to commence a splendid walk downstream, the highlight being an all too brief wooded section. On emerging, note a memorial plate set into a rock that needs to be read carefully. **The path strikes across a field to meet the narrow road at Hough Mill.** Now merely a barn, this ancient building was at one time a corn mill. **Cross the adjacent bridge to leave the road immediately in favour of a rough lane rising to a junction at Howgill Farm.** Just along to the left is Howgill Lodge, where refreshments are usually available.

Cross straight over to continue the climb on a track winding up through plantations to debouch onto open moor, and thus enter the access area. The track now turns left with the wall, rising gently for

a good while before the first of several substantial cairns set the course for a direct strike across the moor. Soon Simon's Seat's crown appears, and the well trodden path reaches it surprisingly quickly. The unmistakable form of an Ordnance Survey column (S5294) adorns the highest rocks, and to add interest to the final few feet, hands must be used to attain it.

At 1592ft, Simon's Seat is a marvellous vantage point, its crest perched above an unbroken plunge to the valley at Skyreholme. This dramatic prospect includes Trollers Gill, Parceval Hall and Grimwith Reservoir - ideal, in fact, for appraising the layout of WALK 22. The distant view, meanwhile, gives a comprehensive picture of the rolling hills in this south-eastern quarter of the National Park. The enormous boulders crowning the top are a first rate playground for the agile, though it must be borne in mind that the great walls of rock falling to the north from the summit are strictly the preserve of rock climbers.

Leave the OS column and retrace steps to the gap between the main cluster of rocks and the lesser outcrops encountered first. Turning right a path drops steeply to a fork. The direct route to Dalehead branches right, but may be closed due to erosion. If it re-opens, slant down to a ladder-stile, then down part-sunken zigzags. Crossing the course of a pipeline, it concludes through trees and bracken to emerge onto Howgill Lane just short of the farm. The waymarked diversion runs to the right, contouring through heather before slanting down to a wall corner. Over a stile at the wall junction below, descend the wall-side to a gate/stile, then go left above a small pinewood to drop down to a farm track. Resume on this as it drops down to Dalehead. Just beyond the farm the direct route joins the farm road.

A little further take a gate on the right, and through it double back to a stile behind a crumbled barn. The way slants down two further fields to a footbridge over Blands Beck, then up a field centre and through a yard onto the road at High Skyreholme. Go left to a junction and keep left through Skyreholme to the next junction by an old chapel. A quick finish is along the lane, but a better one opts for the cruel climb to the right. Just above a barn take a stile on the left: though pathless, no further description is needed. A string of slimline gap-stiles, veritable works of art, offers a fascinating conclusion, and with the cottages of Appletreewick beckoning, just keep an eye on the next stile!

Opposite: The view west from Simon's Seat

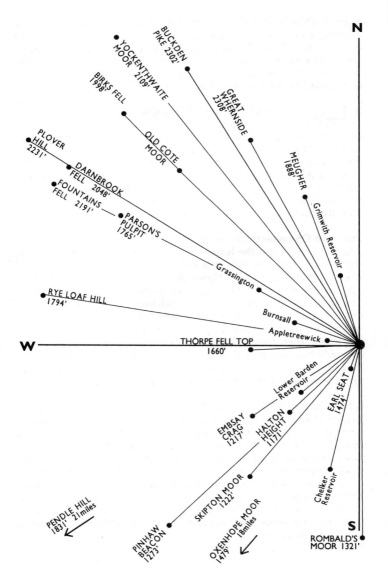

N

BUCKDEN PIKE 2302'

YOCKENTHWAITE MOOR 2109'

GREAT WHERNSIDE 2308'

BIRKS FELL 1998'

OLD COTE MOOR

PLOVER HILL 2231'

DARNBROOK FELL 2048'

MEUGHER 1888'

FOUNTAINS FELL 2191'

PARSON'S PULPIT 1765'

Grimwith Reservoir

Grassington

RYE LOAF HILL 1794'

Burnsall

Appletreewick

W

THORPE FELL TOP 1660'

Lower Barden Reservoir

EARL SEAT 1474'

EMBSAY CRAG 1217'

HALTON HEIGHT 1171'

SKIPTON MOOR 1222'

Chelker Reservoir

PENDLE HILL 1831' 21 miles

PINHAW BEACON 1273'

OXENHOPE MOOR 1479' 18 miles

S

ROMBALD'S MOOR 1321'

29

GRASSINGTON MOOR

START *Grassington*   *Grid ref. SE 002639*

DISTANCE *5¾ miles*

ORDNANCE SURVEY MAPS
1:50,000
Landranger 98 - Wensleydale & Upper Wharfedale
1:25,000
Outdoor Leisure 2 - Yorkshire Dales South/West

ACCESS *Start from the square in the village centre. There is a large National Park car park by the information centre on the Hebden road, and a well sited smaller car park on Moor Lane, behind the old Town Hall. Grassington is served by bus from Skipton.*

Extensive views add to this fine excursion into the environs of the departed lead mining industry.

S Grassington is the undisputed 'capital' of the upper Wharfedale area, a thriving community with a good range of facilities. The fine, cobbled square is the focal point but it is really only the shop window: hidden away is enough interest for a day's leisurely exploration. Historically, Grassington boasted an 18th century theatre and a lead mining industry of which its nearby moor still displays much evidence. The many buildings of character include the Old Hall and the former Town Hall-cum-institute. Here also is the Upper Wharfedale Folk Museum and the headquarters of the fell rescue organisation and the National Park.

From the square take the road up past the *Devonshire Arms* to Town Head. Here turn right along the front of the Town Hall, and take the first left along Low Lane. At the first chance leave this by a rough lane

up to the left, this is High Lane. As it levels out into a pleasant green way, take a gate on the left and follow the next wall up the field to an unobtrusive stile. From here on an indistinct path strikes a diagonal course up through a succession of fields to emerge by a gate onto Edge Lane.

Turning right along it, the walled lane improves into a splendid green way, passing a tall mast before entering a tract of open moor. The track slants up to the left with expanding views across Hebden Gill before the walls close in again. The surprise of seeing a farm (New House) ahead is doubled by the appearance of another, High Garnshaw, in the dip just below. The walled lane (Tinkers' Lane) runs past the latter then climbs close to the former. On it continues, open then enclosed, to drop down to the floor of Hebden Gill.

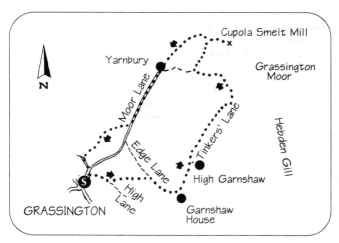

Colourful Hebden Gill was the scene of much mining activity. In the last stage of descent to it, look across into the deep cleft of Bolton Gill to see a dark shadow near to the top. It is a former winding shaft from around 1856, and restored by the Earby Mines Research Group. Turning up the beckside, the track runs through old lead mining remains. At a limekiln the track turns up to the left, climbing through more spoil heaps to a junction with the broad track known as the Duke's New Road.

113

At a gateway just before this point, over to the left is an area of several interesting mining features either side of the wall. The Union Shaft (360ft deep but thankfully covered!) drained into Hebden Gill by the Duke's Level; while the Beever Dam served a crushing mill, and pump and winding gear in the Union Shaft.

At Duke's New Road the main track bears left, aiming directly for Yarnbury past a row of bell-pits. Turning right, however, the track contours around to approach Cupola Smelt Mill. The definitive path on Duke's New Road ends at the stile before the smelt mill. A sign at the mill explains the moor's access situation, though currently the National Park Authority are - understandably - less keen to encourage public access due to the danger from mineshafts and unstable buildings. Visits to the splendid chimney by the obvious line of the flue should be made alongside the flue, and not on it!

Grassington Moor was one of the major centres of lead mining in the Yorkshire Dales, and along with the Pateley Bridge area it rivalled activities in Swaledale. Though dating back to Roman times, the industry reached its peak in the early 19th century, and ended completely before the end of that century. The Cupola Smelt Mill was built in 1793 by the Duke of Devonshire (of course) and was fired by locally won coal. A mile-long system of flues took the fumes from the mill to the chimney via condensors. The chimney itself, at the top of the flue system, was saved and preserved in 1971 by the indefatigable Earby Mines Research Group.

Returning a few yards along the 'road' to cross the infant beck, branch off to the right to locate a stile in a bend in the wall. Here Old Moor Lane is joined, and followed left to become surfaced at Yarnbury. At 1150ft above sea level, the bleak setting of Yarnbury would have been much busier when the site of the mine agent's office.

This traffic-free road, now known simply as Moor Lane, continues all the way down into Grassington. Before the road starts a more purposeful drop, the conclusion can be improved upon by taking up the offer of a stile on the right. After crossing a field the route descends steeply, taking up the company of a wall on the left to reach the head of a green lane, Intake Lane. This leads down to a short-lived snicket onto Chapel Street. Go left to finish.

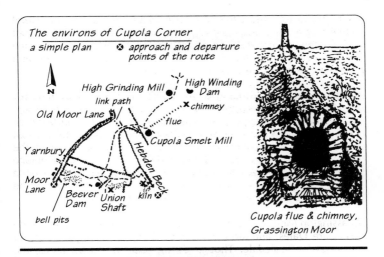

The environs of Cupola Corner
a simple plan   ✪ approach and departure points of the route

High Grinding Mill
High Winding Dam
link path
chimney
Old Moor Lane
flue
Cupola Smelt Mill
Yarnbury
Hebden Beck
Moor Lane
Beever Dam
Union Shaft
kiln
bell pits

Cupola flue & chimney, Grassington Moor

(**30**)

GRIMWITH RESERVOIR

START Grimwith Reservoir   Grid ref. SE 062640

DISTANCE 4¼ miles

ORDNANCE SURVEY MAPS
1:50,000
Landranger 98 - Wensleydale & Upper Wharfedale
            99 - Northallerton & Ripon
1:25,000
Outdoor Leisure 2 - Yorkshire Dales South/West

ACCESS Start from the Water Authority car park signposted off the Grassington-Pateley Bridge road east of Hebden. Hebden is served by bus from Skipton via Grassington.

A very easy circuit offering pleasant views and wildlife. Two sections, in particular the top of the dam, are on permissive paths created by the Water Authority.

S Grimwith Reservoir was constructed in 1884 to supply water to Bradford. As recently as 1983 it was substantially enlarged, making it the largest expanse of inland water in Yorkshire. As a result the old footpath encircling it had to be replaced, either that or swim. In the great drought of 1995 we completed this walk on what could have been the original path, such was the water level. Grimwith is surrounded by rolling moorlands, and in late summer the heather makes a fine backdrop. Part of the reservoir is designated a conservation area, while the greater part is used by a sailing club.

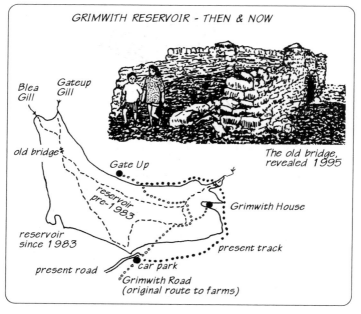

GRIMWITH RESERVOIR - THEN & NOW

Blea Gill

Gateup Gill

old bridge

Gate Up

reservoir pre-1983

reservoir since 1983

present road

car park

Grimwith Road (original route to farms)

The old bridge, revealed 1995

Grimwith House

present track

From the car park take the track at the far (eastern) end from the toilets, which rises to a gate and stile. Just beyond, leave it for a permissive path bearing off to the left. This cuts out a climb on heathery Grimwith Fell, and offers more intimate views over the

shore as it winds along to rejoin the track. On the left here we pass High Laithe Barn, a cruck framed, heather thatched listed building. **On past the farm buildings of Grimwith House and a side dam on the right where Grimwith Beck comes in, the track winds round past a shooting house up to the right and the ruin of Gate Up on the left.** Evidence of mullioned windows suggests that long ago this was a house of some character. Looking across the reservoir, the Barden Moor skyline rises over the dam.

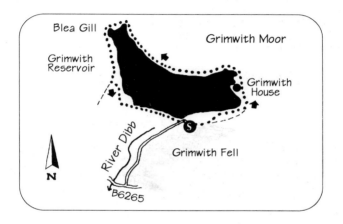

The track finally turns to climb to a barn. **Keeping straight on a footpath takes over, running through bracken to the far corner of the reservoir. This is the finest section as it passes along the foot of two attttractive side gills, Gate Up Gill and Blea Gill.** Again, during the drought, the stone bridge beneath where these two met was uncovered, a curiously isolated structure sat amidst the mud. **The path emerges from the far corner and its bracken as a track returns, leading down the west side now.** There are grand views back into Gate Up Gill and the Grimwith and Appletreewick Moors: ahead, beyond the dam, Simon's Seat now breaks the skyline.

At a fork the return path is sent down to the left, past a barn and then on as a broader track between walls to reach the western end of the great dam. A pleasant walk concludes along the top of the relatively unobtrusive grassy embankment to join the road just short of the car park.

THRESHFIELD MOOR

START Threshfield   Grid ref. SD 989636

DISTANCE 6 miles

ORDNANCE SURVEY MAPS
1:50,000
Landranger 98 - Wensleydale & Upper Wharfedale
1:25,000
Outdoor Leisure 2 - Yorkshire Dales South/West

ACCESS Start from the village green opposite the pub. There is reasonable parking on the adjacent side roads or on the Burnsall road. The pub has a car park for patrons. Threshfield is served by Skipton-Grassington buses.

Heather moorland and limestone delights combine in the relatively unfrequented hinterland of Threshfield

S Threshfield is a disjointed village scattered in various directions around the junction of the Skipton-Grassington road with the main updale road. The 'new' part of the village - with its striking Catholic church of modern design - is along the road towards Grassington, but it is the more interesting old corner we visit. Solid stone cottages overlook a quaint, triangular green, enclosed by walls and shrouded in trees. Inside are some stocks and the flowers of spring. Alongside the green a stone lintel dated 1651 identifies the old Post office. Just across the main road is the popular *Old Hall* inn, whose title serves to indicate its original purpose. The village school stands down by the river, a former grammar school dating from the 17th century.

Leave the village by heading south along the main road, over Threshfield Bridge and up the hill behind to quickly escape by a narrow road on the right. Moor Lane rises steadily to lose its surface

at a junction before continuing up to a gate onto the moor. Of the departing tracks take the right-hand one, which curves round before climbing steadily. In evidence nearby is the site of a former colliery, where poor quality coal was won to fuel the lead smelting operations on Grassington Moor.

Our firm track facilitates rapid progress up through the heather of Threshfield Moor. As a string of stone shooting butts take shape on the left, the track is vacated as it swings up to the right: our less discernible way contours straight ahead, passing between the butts to run on to an obvious wall junction ahead.

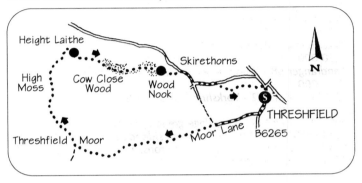

At the wall turn right to remain on the moor, and at the first opportunity our way enters a walled section through which it runs as a splendid green lane. This provides glimpses first of Winterburn Reservoir and then of the limestone uplands of Malham Moor. At the far end is a return to open moor, the less than dry crossing of High Moss being aided by marker posts. At 1235ft, High Moss is the highest point of the walk.

Slowly descending, an intervening fence is crossed before the path drops to a gate. Here limestone country is re-entered, with a short section between walls. Before reaching a barn (with a splendidly preserved limekiln behind), the track is left through the collapsed wall on the right, behind which a stile precedes a wall-side descent to the working barn of Height Laithe. Looking east to a prominent knoll, note the twin dark entrances of Calf Hole (also known as Height Cave). Important evidence of occupation by Bronze and Iron age man has been yielded here.

From a stile at the bottom, enter the yard and turn right up a walled track. Near the top turn left through a gap and head away with the left-hand wall. Marker posts are again in evidence to guide the way to the far corner of the pasture to drop down to Height House. Passing left of the barn a stile will be located near a gate at the end of the field, and on the other side a clear path leads on to the right into Cow Close Wood. This section is an absolute joy, tracing the infant Rowley Beck down through a scattered natural woodland below limestone outcrops. Oak, ash and thorn are interlaced with boulders deposited by the glaciers, while bluebells add spring colour. At the bottom a stile admits to Wood Nook caravan site, this course maintained down the drive, past the house and out onto Wood Lane.

Turn down the narrow road into Skirethorns. Skirethorns boasts a chocolate box scene of cottages across a tiny green: shame about the quarry. At a junction with a wide and dusty quarry road, escape is quickly effected by means of a stile on the right. A seldom trodden path with stiles at all the right places now leads back into Threshfield, firstly by crossing to the opposite corner, then bearing right around the bottom of two fields, a choice presents itself. The fact that Threshfield's hostelry merits its own guidepost might be sufficient incentive to follow the wall away. Crossing it part way along, when the wall turns away rise up the field to the corner in front of the houses. A brace of stiles precede emergence alongside the *Old Hall*.

The Old Hall, Threshfield

*Limekiln above
Height Laithe*

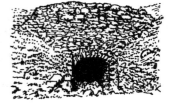

32

BIRKS FELL RIDGE

START   Buckden   **Grid ref. SD 942772**

DISTANCE   11 miles

ORDNANCE SURVEY MAPS
1:50,000
Landranger 98 - Wensleydale & Upper Wharfedale
1:25,000
Outdoor Leisure 30 - Yorkshire Dales North/Central

ACCESS   Start from the village centre. There is a large National
Park car park. Buckden is served by occasional bus from Skipton
via Grassington and by seasonal Dalesbus.

A strenuous inter-valley double crossing, but a classic. Two valley
floor sections through lush pastures contrast with delectable crossings
from Wharfedale to Littondale and back. Magnificent views, and a
village (and pub!) at all four corners.

S   Buckden is the first sizeable settlement encountered by the
Wharfe, and stands at the meeting place of two high roads from
Wensleydale to the north. The good quality B6160 comes via Cray to
take over as the valley road from the narrow, winding strip of tarmac
that reaches nearly 2000 feet on its way over Fleet Moss from Hawes,
before running through Langstrothdale to Buckden. In medieval times
Buckden was the centre of a vast hunting forest, and its hostelry recalls
its former importance in its name. The village stands high above the
river on the slopes of Buckden Pike, and swift-flowing Buckden Beck
carves a deep defile down from the summit.

**Leave the village by descending the Hawes road and over the bridge.
Continue a little further then go left along the first farm drive. Over
the cattle-grid, take the right branch zigzagging up the field above**

121

**Redmire Farm. At the top corner the track passes through sheep pens
and onto the foot of the open fell. It runs along to the left through
limestone scenery, then at a fork turns right to begin the main climb.**
High above, the moorland skyline awaits. The views back feature the
huddle of Buckden nestling beneath the pike, with the defile of
Buckden Beck linking the two.

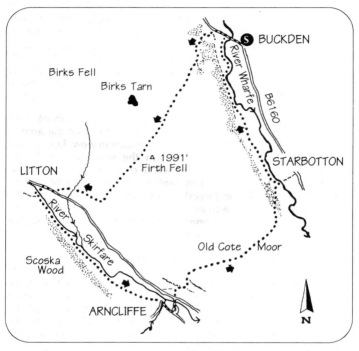

**The path is largely good and the marker posts largely superfluous as
it slants steadily up the hill. Peatier ground is encountered as height
is gained.** Though not difficult to walk, a lengthy section of this is
causing concern as the soft ground has fallen victim to erosion.
Unfortunately this is not helped by its classification as a bridleway, but
nevertheless please tread carefully to avoid undue exacerbation.
Quite effortlessly the edge of the broad ridge top is soon gained. Out
of sight less than half a mile along to the right is the secretive Birks
Tarn, a large sheet of water for its near-2000ft altitude.

A crumbling wall is joined and quickly passed through a gateway, followed a while then a corner cut to join the sturdy ridge wall. Go left with this (a good windbreak) a couple of minutes to a gate at a junction. This is the summit of the walk, the crossing of the mighty Birks Fell ridge. At 2001ft Birks Fell was long regarded as the most innocuous of Yorkshire's mountains, but modern mapping has cruelly demoted it below the magical contour. The highest point is an imperceptible rise further to the north-west. The ridge stretches over 11 miles from Knipe Scar in the east to an arbitrary conclusion in Ribblesdale, beyond the wilds of Cosh. Over to the left, meanwhile, are the marginally lower cairn and OS column at 1991ft on Firth Fell, just one of many named fells that constitute the full ridge. Looking ahead, eyes are quickly drawn to Penyghent rearing its mighty frame across Upper Littondale: now that is unquestionably a mountain!

Through the gate follow the wall off the ridge top, a short level section preceding the long descent. This is steeper than the ascent, with glorious views over the dale, and Litton itself in view. **Leaving the heather moor it continues down with the wall through lusher terrain. Part-way, it loops off to the left to curve back to finally pass through the wall at a gate. It then slants away alongside a redundant hollowed way with Litton directly ahead. The track fades along the bottom edge of a pasture to arrive at a footbridge crossing Crystal Beck. The green walled way opposite quickly slants down to emerge in Litton just yards short of the inn.**

Though secondary to Arncliffe, Litton can boast that it gave its name to the valley once known as Amerdale. Its attractive buildings are strung along the road from the unspoilt, whitewashed *Queens Arms*. If it's open, this one will take some passing! **From the inn head on through the village and leave the road just beyond the telephone box, down a drive to the left immediately before two barns usher the road out of Litton. Bear left of a short wall to a narrow wooden footbridge over the river Skirfare.**

The river is regularly dry here, the Skirfare having gone subterranean some distance upstream. **Turn downstream to a stile, then cross an enclosure to the next stile. Turn right alongside a tiny stream, crossing it at a bridge onto a drive. Go left a few yards then take a gate on the right. Cross the field to a gate to the right, opposite, then go left with the wall, continuing straight on to a corner gate to rejoin the river. A narrow, confined path squeezes downstream, finally emerging at a gate to resume through the fields.**

Though at times faint underfoot, the way is largely clear as it heads on through the fields, generally keeping between the river and the base of the slope to the right. At a bend of the river (probably still dry) we pass along the foot of the extensive Scoska Wood. The Dales' largest surviving natural ash woodland has been designated as a National Nature Reserve in recognition of its importance. **Leaving the reserve, it's back to the field centres, soon crossing a massive pasture which is left by a stile on a projecting corner to the left just short of the end. From the next stile a walled track is joined: this leads unerringly into Arncliffe, not seen until we are virtually in it!**

Cross the road bridge in front to enter the village green. Arncliffe is one of the most attractive yet least spoilt villages in the Dales, and is regarded as the 'capital' of Littondale. A variety of characterful greystone houses stand back in relaxed manner from a spacious green. The unpretentious inn, the *Falcon*, maintains this mood, and is the only hostelry in the area to serve its ale in that unrivalled fashion, directly from the barrel. On joining the green note a 1730 datestone on the left, while just short of the phone box a 1677 datestone adorns a barn. A tiny Post office still survives here, while there is also a tearoom round the corner.

Out of sight of the green is St.Oswald's church, which has found its own niche embowered in trees in a truly beautiful riverside setting. Though largely rebuilt last century, the solid tower dates back 500 years. Inside is a list of the Littondale men who marched off to fight at Flodden Field in 1513. Across the shapely bridge, the house at Bridge End played host to Charles Kingsley during his *Water Babies* period.

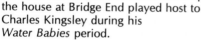

Buckden Bridge

Leave by the Litton (up-dale) road, passing the church and crossing the bridge over the Skirfare. Note the return of the river, thanks to springs further upstream. **At the junction at the end, take a stile in front and climb a couple of steep fields to join a broad track.** The retrospective views over the village, up Cowside Beck and down Littondale are outstanding. **The track winds up through the limestone shelves of Park Scar and Brayshaw Scar, and along to a gateway onto a grand tract of heather moorland. Ignore the fork left to the prominent shooting box, and enjoy the track's climb through the sea of heather.**

Suddenly it levels out and the ridge wall on Old Cote Moor is just ahead. It can be seen descending for some way down to the right, while in front Buckden Pike and Great Whernside appear majestically, a stunning prospect. **Pass through the gate and head directly away on the wall-side path. At the wall corner pass through and continue directly down, the path becoming a little faint just above a wall where it drops left to pass through a gateway in it. Continue straight down, passing round the left side of a crumbling circular enclosure to find a gate and guideposts at the wall below. Turn through it to earn an exhilarating arrival atop a steep drop to the valley.**

Buckden Pike oversees a very complete picture culminating in the strikingly flat dale floor, with the three villages having returned more fully. Best positioned is Starbotton, from where Cam Gill Beck strikes deep into the flank of the pike. **The way slants gently away from the wall before commencing a steeper, sunken drop into an old wood. It slants all the way down, emerging at the bottom between hoary, lichen-covered walls. By a barn at the bottom it swings right to a footbridge over the Wharfe.**

The track across it offers a detour up to the road in Starbotton (see WALK 10). **Don't cross the bridge unless visiting Starbotton but turn left to follow the river upstream to return to Buckden. When the Wharfe temporarily parts company the path continues straight ahead alongside a wall on the left: several stiles and gates interrupt the journey. As the river returns a wide track is joined, but as the Wharfe bends away again this time go with it to remain on its bank until Buckden Bridge is encountered. Here leave the river and cross the bridge to re-enter the village.**

LOG OF THE WALKS

WALK	DATE	NOTES
1		
2		
3		
4		
5		
6		
7		
8		
9		
10		
11		
12		
13		
14		
15		
16		

LOG OF THE WALKS

WALK	DATE	NOTES
17		
18		
19		
20		
21		
22		
23		
24		
25		
26		
27		
28		
29		
30		
31		
32		

INDEX

Principal features: walk number refers

Appletreewick	7,8,28	Kettlewell	5,10,16,18,24
Arncliffe	5,32	Kilnsey	27
		Kilnsey Crag	27
Barden	14,17		
Barden Moor	15,17	Langcliffe Edge	24
Bastow Wood	19	Langerton Hill	7
Beckermonds	26	Lea Green	19
Birks Fell	32	Linton	2,15
Bolton Abbey	1,11,14,20	Linton Falls	2,4,21
Bolton Bridge	11	Litton	9,32
Bordley	27		
Buckden	3,23,25,32	Mastiles Lane	27
Buckden Pike	25		
Burnsall	7,21	Old Cote Moor	5,10,32
Capplestone Gate	6	Parceval Hall	8,22
Conistone	6,19	Penyghent Gill	9
Conistone Dib	6,19	Providence Pot	16
Cosh	12		
Cracoe	15	Simon's Seat	1,28
Cracoe Fell	15	Skirethorns	31
Cray	3	Skirfare, river	5,9,12,32
		Skyreholme	8,22,28
Deepdale	26	Starbotton	10,18,25,32
Dibb, river	7,22,30	Storiths	20
		Strid, The	14
Foxup	12	Strid Wood	14
		Stump Cross Caverns	22
Grassington	4,19,29		
Grassington Moor	29	Thorpe	15,21
Grass Wood	4	Thorpe Fell Top	15
Great Whernside	16	Threshfield	2,31
Grimwith Reservoir	22,30	Threshfield Moor	31
		Trollers Gill	8,22
Halton Gill	12,26		
Hawkswick	5	Valley of Desolation	1
Hazlewood Moor	20		
Hebden	13,21	Wharfe, river	1,2,3,4,5,7,8,10,11,14
Hebden Gill	13		17,18,19,20,21,23,24,25,26,27,28,32
Horse Head Pass	26		
Howgill	8,28	Yarnbury	29
Hubberholme	3,23	Yockenthwaite	23,26